Writing
Matters
in Every Classroom

Writing
Matters
in Every Classroom

Angela Peery, Ed.D.

LEAD+
LEARN
PRESS

The Leadership and Learning Center
317 Inverness Way South, Suite 150
Englewood, Colorado 80112
Phone 1.866.399.6019 | Fax 303.504.9417
LeadandLearn.com

Published by Lead+Learn Press, a division of Advanced Learning Centers, Inc.

11 10 09 08 01 02 03 04 05 06 07 08 09

Cover photo: Purestock/Getty Images

ISBN 978-1-933196-79-4

Library of Congress Cataloging-in-Publication Data

Peery, Angela B., 1964-
    Writing matters in every classroom / Angela Peery.
        p. cm.
    Includes bibliographical references and index.
    ISBN 978-1-933196-79-4 (alk. paper)
    1. Composition (Language arts) I. Title.
    LB1575.8.P43 2009
    372.62'3—dc22
                                2009002601

Contents

List of Exhibits

Acknowledgments

No book reaches the publication stage without a great deal of behind-the-scenes help and intellectual sparks from others. I'm deeply grateful to my colleagues at The Leadership and Learning Center, especially Laura Benson, Laura Besser, Juan Cordova, Brandon Doubek, Martha Fenstermacher, Tracey Flach, Linda Gregg, Mike Nobel, and Doug Reeves, all of whom have moved this project forward at critical points.

Working with teachers across the country as they have implemented increased nonfiction writing in their classrooms has also helped me immeasurably. I especially thank the Writing-to-Learn certified trainers in the Northwest Regional Education Service District, Oregon, and in the Sierra Vista Public Schools, Arizona. Teachers from the Savannah–Chatham Public Schools in Georgia, Waterloo Middle School in New York, and Elkhart Public Schools in Indiana have also helped shape my thinking.

I am especially indebted to Dianne Nelson for her compassionate editing. Every writer should be fortunate enough to experience editing that helps clarify one's words and still makes one feel understood and valued.

When I'm not in schools, working with teachers and administrators, I'm home trying to distill my copious notes into materials (like this book) that I hope are of benefit to others. During these times, it's my husband, Tim, who is subjected to my procrastination and deadline-induced panic. For always being steady and supportive, I thank him and promise that when I write the next book, I'll do better.

About the Author

 **Dr. Angela Peery** is a Senior Professional Development Associate at The Leadership and Learning Center and is a teacher, researcher, and writer. Just before joining the Center, she worked for the South Carolina Department of Education as an instructional coach at a low-achieving middle school and helped raise student proficiency in writing. Previously, she was also a literacy consultant for the National Urban Alliance for Effective Education, working with teachers in high-poverty schools in Seattle and Indianapolis.

Dr. Peery's experience includes ten years of classroom teaching at the secondary level, four years as a high school assistant principal, and various curriculum leadership roles at the building, district, and state levels. She has taught graduate education courses at Coastal Carolina University and the University of Phoenix Online and is a co-director of a National Writing Project site. She has also taught undergraduate composition for Horry–Georgetown Technical College and Kaplan University Online.

In 2000, Dr. Peery earned her doctorate in curriculum and instruction. During her dissertation research phase of almost two years, she worked with a Jewish day school to improve literacy instruction. She is the author of two books, *Deep Change: Professional Development from the Inside Out* and *ARRIVE: Improving Instruction through Reflective Journaling*. Additional seminars and materials related to literacy, especially vocabulary acquisition and nonfiction writing, are currently being developed for the Center.

Dr. Peery is a native of Salem, Virginia, and holds degrees from Randolph–Macon Woman's College, Hollins College, and the University of South Carolina. Her professional licensures include secondary English, secondary administration, and gifted/talented education.

Her family consists of husband Tim, three Labrador retrievers, and a cat. They currently reside on Lady's Island in the Beaufort/Hilton Head area of South Carolina. Angela is an officer in her homeowners' association and works with a local citizens' school-improvement group. In her spare time, she enjoys leisure travel and entertaining friends and family.

Dr. Peery can be reached at APeery@LeadandLearn.com.

CHAPTER 1

What's So Important About Nonfiction Writing?

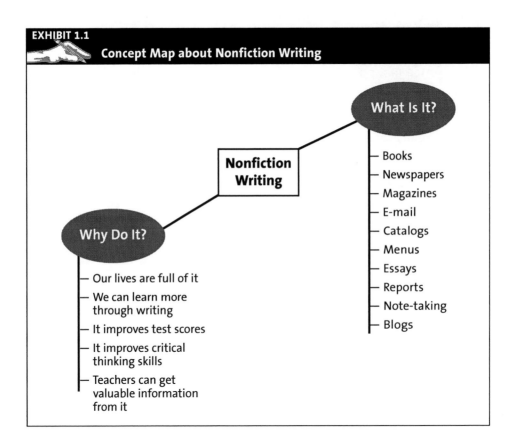

EXHIBIT 1.1

Concept Map about Nonfiction Writing

What Is It?

Nonfiction Writing

— Books
— Newspapers
— Magazines
— E-mail
— Catalogs
— Menus
— Essays
— Reports
— Note-taking
— Blogs

Why Do It?

— Our lives are full of it
— We can learn more through writing
— It improves test scores
— It improves critical thinking skills
— Teachers can get valuable information from it

What have you read—for work, during leisure time, as related to the needs of your family, and so on—within the last forty-eight hours? Take a moment to think. If you were to list the materials you've read, would your list be similar to mine, below?

- E-mail from colleagues and clients
- Local newspaper
- Online weather reports and maps
- Online news and entertainment reports

- Fashion magazine
- News magazine
- Catalogs
- Professional books for work
- Instructions for a new appliance
- Mail
- Bank statement
- Restaurant menus
- PowerPoint presentations and accompanying handouts

What do you notice about my list? All of the items are functional, aren't they? Each item is related to what I needed in order to stay informed, run a household, or do my job well. None of the items seem particularly literary, do they? In a broad sense, they would all be classified as "nonfiction."

Approximately 85 percent of the reading we do as adults is of nonfiction materials (Stead 2001), and my list mirrors this fact. Certainly there are days when I read various forms of literature (especially during my annual vacation in Mexico), including poetry, one of my favorite genres. However, most of my days, like the days of many other adults in 2008, are filled with nonfiction texts that help me work, take care of myself, nurture others, relax, and even entertain myself.

Literary reading is on the decline, it seems. The National Endowment for the Arts reported in its 2004 study *Reading at Risk: A Survey of Literary Reading* that in the 17,000 U.S. households surveyed, literary reading (novels, short stories, poetry, and plays) was falling in popularity. Fewer than half of those American adults surveyed now read literature *at all*. The report also notes declines for all groups studied, with the steepest rate (28 percent) occurring in the youngest age group. (The report is available free for download at http://www.arts.gov/pub/ReadingAtRisk.pdf.) As a former high school and college English teacher, these statistics disturb me, but I know anecdotally that they are accurate.

I am certainly not arguing for any of us to read *less* literature. Literature allows us to understand the human condition more fully, and a good story, poem, or play resonates with us long after we've experienced it. However, it's a fact of our twenty-first-century lives that we read tons of nonfiction—all day, every day. In schools, students need to work with literary texts, to be sure—but we also need to prepare them to read and write various forms of nonfiction competently.

This book shows how we, as teachers, can orchestrate increased nonfiction writing in our classrooms and, by so doing, *raise student achievement in all subject areas*. Here you'll find strategies to help you use more nonfiction writing with your students, no matter what subject you're teaching at any given time. You'll also find ideas about how to assess writing quickly, fairly, and accurately. Quality assessment helps you provide feedback to students so that they become increasingly competent writers and also learn content-area material more effectively. Writing (connected to content) provides students the "double whammy" of increased subject understanding and greater writing proficiency.

Why We Need to Increase the Amount of Nonfiction Writing

Obviously, nonfiction texts like online information, newspapers, and magazines are abundant in our lives. Being a competent reader of these materials is important, but this in itself is not a compelling argument for having students *write* more nonfiction.

Credible research over decades makes a simple statement: Writing enhances learning. (If you are interested in further study on this subject, references are provided in this book.)

Having nonfiction writing skills is linked to higher achievement.

Does the following experience sound familiar to you? When I had to write a paper in college, I had to prove to my professor that I knew what I was talking about. I had to seek evidence to prove my points, whether the paper was a literary analysis, a discussion of a controversial historical event, or a research report on an influential person or scientific phenomenon. Sitting passively, listening to lectures, taking notes, and performing well on tests were easier to "fake" than creating original prose. If you've ever written and defended a master's thesis or dissertation, you know exactly how these assignments required you to know your subject matter deeply. It's difficult to write something of substance without knowing the subject well; conversely, it's hard to write about something well without learning it even better.

Having nonfiction writing skills is also linked to higher achievement. One study correlated higher achievement in science with increased writing (Klentschy, Garrison, and Amaral 2000). A four-year study of fourth- and sixth-graders funded by the National Science Foundation found that the experimental group scored significantly higher than the control group, which did not experience writing in its science classes. In fact, writing not only improved science achievement but also raised test scores in other subject areas. Similarly, students who did significant writing in college history classes improved their writing and demonstrated greater historical accuracy (Nussbaum, Kardash, and Graham 2005). We can see that writing not only creates better writers, but perhaps better historians. A meta-analysis of forty-eight published studies about writing across the curriculum (elementary through college) examined the relationship between classroom writing-to-learn activities and student achievement (Bangert-Drowns, Hurley, and Wilkinson 2004). The researchers concluded that writing-to-learn activities can have a positive impact on conventional measures of academic achievement (page 29). The use of metacognitive prompts—those in which students "reflect on their current knowledge, confusions, and learning processes"—proved highly effective (page 50). The longer the period of time over which writing activities were spread and repeated, the greater the effect was on student learning.

Some school systems have achieved large-scale achievement. One such success story is the Riverview Gardens School District in Missouri. Its "Write Focus" program includes collaboratively scored writing assessments for every class (even music, physical education, and art) on a monthly basis. Using common rubrics among all teachers, the district tripled the number of students who scored proficient or better in writing in only two years. This "diversion" of time and effort from other subjects had another interesting consequence: dramatic increases in state test scores in science and social studies (Reeves 2000).

Norfolk Public Schools in Virginia was awarded the 2005 Broad Prize for being the highest performing urban school system in the country and consistently shows a positive correlation between increased nonfiction writing and high test scores. Back in 1998, when their clear focus on increased achievement was just beginning, educators first implemented more writing across the curriculum. Exhibit 1.2 shows their early but impressive results correlating writing/language arts test scores with those in other tested subjects.

EXHIBIT 1.2

Correlations Between Increased Writing and Test Scores in Other Subjects

3rd Grade English Correlation	5th Grade Writing Correlation	8th Grade Writing Correlation
Math = .88	Math = .77	Math = .83
History = .87	History = .75	History = .79
Science = .86	Science = .85	Science = .86

Norfolk has sustained its high achievement and continues to use cross-curricular writing for all grade levels. The system employs common writing rubrics that help *all* teachers provide consistent scoring and feedback so that students continuously improve.

On a smaller scale, one school in South Carolina accomplished tremendous success by focusing on writing. Woodland High School went from the state's "academic watch" list to receiving an excellent improvement rating, and their average SAT score rose twenty-two points—in just one year! This happened because the following strategies were implemented:

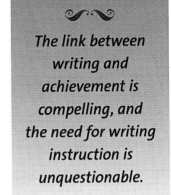

The link between writing and achievement is compelling, and the need for writing instruction is unquestionable.

- Monthly common writing assessments, each focusing on a different content area

- Weekly written products in all content areas, as determined by teachers

- Collaborative scoring of papers, which helped teachers provide consistent expectations

- Data transparency, with class and school results posted clearly for all to see in the main hall of the building.

A high school geometry teacher with whom I've worked in Madera County, California, started adding a writing component to his classes and found that increasingly higher rates of students began passing the unit tests. A middle school science teacher who is a personal friend started using written summaries in her classes about five years ago and has seen her students retain more science content and perform better on unit tests, exams, and standardized tests. A middle school that you'll read about later in this book achieved dramatic success with a school-wide writing initiative. In just a little more than a year, after having four consecutive years of low achievement, the school was removed from the state "watch list."

The link between writing and achievement is compelling, and the need for writing instruction is unquestionable. A 2007 meta-analysis of almost 600 studies (Graham and Perin) concluded that writing is essential for adolescents. Students without adequate writing skills suffer disadvantages in multiple subjects in school and later in the job market. This study also found that student writing is inadequate. Many students fail to meet grade-level standards in writing, and more than half of all students entering college are not prepared for the kinds of writing they are expected to do. Businesses spend more than $3 billion annually on writing remediation. Only more writing in America's classrooms can remedy these problems!

Simply put, America's students need to learn to write better. Eighty percent of fourth- and eighth-graders taking the 2002 National Assessment of Educational Progress writing test scored only in the basic range (http://nces.ed.gov/nationsreportcard/writing/). Sadly, no significant change in the performance of twelfth-graders was detected. These data speak volumes about the need to challenge our students with meaningful writing assignments right up until graduation day.

> *Americans believe good writing skills are more important than ever.*

Several prominent national groups and professional organizations have been quite public about their wishes that K-12 students be asked to write more. The National Commission on Writing, in its initial report to Congress, said that a "writing revolution" is necessary to put writing in its proper, prominent place in the classroom so that education can become an "engine of opportunity and economic growth" (http://www.writingcommission.org/prod_downloads/writingcom/neglectedr.pdf). The report goes on to say that writing is the way students "connect the dots" in their learning and makes a forceful argument that good writing is essential to success in the workplace. A recent study by the National Writing Project indicated that Americans believe that good writing skills are more important than ever (http://www.nwp.org/cs/public/print/resource/2389). Two-thirds of the public would like to see more resources invested in helping teachers teach writing, and 74 percent think that writing should be taught in all subjects and at all grade levels.

The position statement of the National Council of Teachers of English (NCTE) closely aligns with the views of the National Commission on Writing. NCTE recognizes that writing fosters learning in all disciplines (http://www.ncte.org/edpolicy/writing/research/122398.htm) and recommends frequent writing practice in *all subject areas.*

What Should We, as Teachers, Do?

If we believe that we need to integrate more writing into our classrooms, what kinds of writing should we assign, exactly? Generally, when teachers discuss cross-curricular writing, two broad terms are used: writing-to-learn (sometimes called expressive writing) and learning-to-write (sometimes called product writing). *Writing-to-learn* activities and assignments are designed more for a metacognitive effect. These are forms of writing in which it is most important for students to record their ideas, reflect upon their own learning, and grapple with

Written Reflections

Reasons to Have My Students Do More Writing:	Questions and Concerns I Have at This Point:

unfamiliar content. When students create writing-to-learn texts, the goal is fc them to learn more deeply. The emphasis is on content, and not on form or cor ventions. *Learning-to-write* activities, however, result in more polished products– the academic essay, the research report, and so on. These written products mu show content-area learning plus competency in a particular written form.

Using both writing-to-learn and learning-to-write activities is beneficial, ar this book will address both broad categories. Many teachers find that they fir grow comfortable with using writing-to-learn activities and then move into hel ing students craft more polished products. This kind of cross-curricular "easi into" writing may be a perfect fit for you. If you are part of a collaborative tea that is tackling writing, or if you have extensive experience with using learning-to-write assignments already, you may able to utilize learning-to-write activities immediately. Whatever your situation, though, simply adding more non- fiction writing to your curriculum will benefit your students tremendously.

Adding nonfiction v your curric(benefit you(tremenc

One of the best reminders about why students must write more comes from respected educator and author Lucy Calkins in 1994: "When students do short stints of writing, it can switch their brains from off to on. It can nudge them to question, summ rize, notice, categorize" (page 489). Let's think about how to switch our stude brains "on" as we continue to explore the various applications of nonfiction w ing in our classrooms.

Next you'll find a place where you may do your own writing. This is to you organize your thoughts and concerns about incorporating more nonfic writing into your classroom. You will find an invitation to write at the end of chapter.

unfamiliar content. When students create writing-to-learn texts, the goal is for them to learn more deeply. The emphasis is on content, and not on form or conventions. *Learning-to-write* activities, however, result in more polished products—the academic essay, the research report, and so on. These written products must show content-area learning plus competency in a particular written form.

Using both writing-to-learn and learning-to-write activities is beneficial, and this book will address both broad categories. Many teachers find that they first grow comfortable with using writing-to-learn activities and then move into helping students craft more polished products. This kind of cross-curricular "easing into" writing may be a perfect fit for you. If you are part of a collaborative team that is tackling writing, or if you have extensive experience with using learning-to-write assignments already, you may able to utilize learning-to-write activities immediately. Whatever your situation, though, simply adding more non-fiction writing to your curriculum will benefit your students tremendously.

> *Adding more nonfiction writing to your curriculum will benefit your students tremendously.*

One of the best reminders about why students must write more comes from respected educator and author Lucy Calkins in 1994: "When students do short stints of writing, it can switch their brains from off to on. It can nudge them to question, summarize, notice, categorize" (page 489). Let's think about how to switch our students' brains "on" as we continue to explore the various applications of nonfiction writing in our classrooms.

Next you'll find a place where you may do your own writing. This is to help you organize your thoughts and concerns about incorporating more nonfiction writing into your classroom. You will find an invitation to write at the end of each chapter.

Written Reflections

Reasons to Have My Students Do More Writing:	Questions and Concerns I Have at This Point:

CHAPTER 2

The Basics of the Writing Process

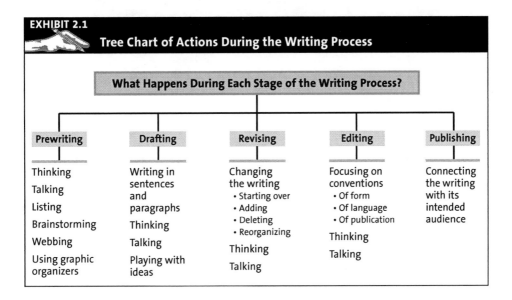

EXHIBIT 2.1

Tree Chart of Actions During the Writing Process

What Happens During Each Stage of the Writing Process?

Prewriting	Drafting	Revising	Editing	Publishing
Thinking	Writing in sentences and paragraphs	Changing the writing	Focusing on conventions	Connecting the writing with its intended audience
Talking		• Starting over	• Of form	
Listing		• Adding	• Of language	
Brainstorming	Thinking	• Deleting	• Of publication	
Webbing	Talking	• Reorganizing	Thinking	
Using graphic organizers	Playing with ideas	Thinking	Talking	
		Talking		

You may not have extensive training or experience in teaching writing. Never fear! You can still create meaningful writing assignments for your students and provide guidance as students benefit from the writing process in your classroom.

Ah, the writing process. We, as educators, hear about it all the time, but do we really understand it? What is it, exactly? It's time to discuss critical vocabulary that we will need for the remainder of this "crash course" on teaching writing. Most educators, writers, and researchers recognize the following names for the five stages of the writing process:

Prewriting

Drafting

Revising

Editing

Publishing

These stages do not necessarily occur in a linear fashion. They can overlap, double back on each other, and have other kinds of relationships depending on the uniqueness of each writer and on the nature of the writing task. Exhibit 2.2 represents the cyclical nature of the process well.

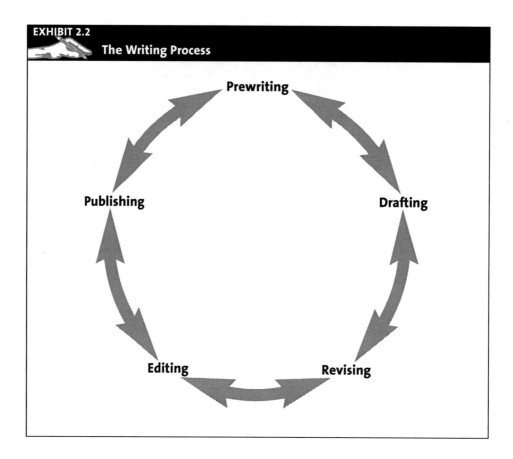

EXHIBIT 2.2

The Writing Process

You may understand the recursive nature of the writing process from your own experiences, but it's worth remembering that, unlike the order of operations in mathematics or verb declensions in a foreign language, the steps in the writing process do not necessarily proceed in a set order. If, as a teacher, you try to enforce a strictly linear process with your students, you will inhibit them from achieving all that they possibly can in their writing.

Let's discuss each stage briefly.

Prewriting

Generally, with any new piece of writing that will undergo repeated drafts, the process begins at a stage known as "prewriting." Prewriting can look very different for each writer.

Prewriting includes activities in which students think about, gather, and organize ideas. Various actions can occur in this stage, including list-making, free writing, using graphic organizers, outlining, brainstorming, and even talking with other writers. Prewriting is not a single act in isolation—although it can be, depending on the individual writer's needs and preferences and the given task. Some writers may even begin their earliest drafts in forms that end up being very close to what the final product will be. (I'm that type of writer myself, and have been since fourth grade.) You may see this particular kind of student writing very little initially, or very little until the last minute (which can be infuriating for you)—but it is the way that many students work, especially as they grow more comfortable with the academic writing tasks assigned to them.

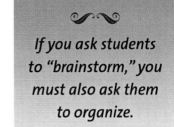

If you ask students to "brainstorm," you must also ask them to organize.

Prewriting is not simply "brainstorming," as some teachers inaccurately describe it. Brainstorming consists of generating as many ideas as possible, without restraint. Brainstorming can indeed be an early step in prewriting, but the multitude of ideas created must later be organized somehow. Therefore, if you ask students to "brainstorm," you must also ask them to organize. That would be two distinct steps in the prewriting stage. *Remember the two main components of prewriting: generating and organizing.* The stage is not usually just one of these.

Akin to brainstorming is *webbing*, a prewriting strategy in which students are encouraged to write a topic within a circle in the center of their paper and then generate supporting ideas in other circles around this central idea. The resulting visual will look similar to a concept map. Like pure brainstorming, webbing can be quite random. If students aren't shown how to organize information from a web, they will not be able to draft well after the web is created.

Thinking about your own prewriting strategies may help you better understand some of the strategies used by your students. When you have to write a letter to parents, a grant application, or an announcement to be read on the school loudspeaker, how do you begin? Do you start with a list or outline and then write from that? Do you freely start writing in a conversational style and then go back to cut parts out and rework other parts? Do you talk your ideas through with someone before writing anything? Or do you attempt to draft in complete sentences and ideas first, similar to the final product? Does your prewriting process change depending on the length and complexity of the piece, or based on the audience that will be receiving the message, or a combination of these factors (and perhaps others, too)? Reflecting on your own prewriting processes may help you find ways to help your students refine theirs. At the very least, talk with your students about your prewriting strategies. This kind of thinking aloud will help them find their own effective methods.

> ☙☙
>
> *Reflecting on your own prewriting processes may help you find ways to help your students refine theirs.*

Remember: Prewriting gets a student thinking, planning, and shaping ideas.

It's okay for a piece of writing to stop at the prewriting stage. Perhaps the student has not found a workable idea, or is not happy with the organizational plan, and has other ideas from which to select. Or you may ask students to do lots of prewriting and "exploration"-type activities before assigning drafting to give them plenty of practice with generating and organizing ideas. In both of these cases, and in other classroom situations, not going beyond the prewriting stage is acceptable.

Drafting

In many cases, the next stage of the writing process is drafting, or efforts to write the first version of the product. Nancie Atwell, a widely respected writing teacher, and a writer herself, encourages her students to draft in paragraphs (only when the assignment calls for prose, obviously). I have found this to be good advice for my own writing and for working with middle school and high school students. Jim Burke, a high school English teacher and author of excellent professional development books, frequently argues that mastering the paragraph is the essence of good writing. Writing strong paragraphs is indeed an important skill, and a prerequisite for students to write effective academic essays. However, even if the form of writing is something different from the traditional essay or report, it's important to encourage students to embrace the assigned form early in the drafting process. As Atwell often says, we should want students to write "the best way they know how" when they are beginning to work on what will become the final product (Atwell 1998).

One way to think about drafting is to use athletic metaphors. This example may also work with your students to help them understand the drafting stage: "If I were a tennis player, all of my practice would be important as I started my first match of a tournament. A draft is like that match. I've prepared; now it's time to play. The 'playing' is the drafting."

Here is another sports metaphor: "I was a competitive gymnast in my youth. I had practice sessions after school every day during competition season, and for years, I also had weekly private lessons. Those practice sessions were like prewriting: I was planning for my performances, organizing my moves, and experimenting with new feats. The competitions against other school teams or other gymnastics clubs were like written drafts. When my team made it to regional tournaments, those resembled revised and edited drafts; I was delivering my most polished performances, hoping that these 'published pieces' would propel my team to first place."

A golf metaphor may also be useful: "The work on putting and driving, plus all of the reflecting on good shots versus bad shots, and all of the planning of future games, are a lot like prewriting. Combining those skills and playing eighteen holes is like a draft. And then, when you play against friends or in a tournament, that's more like a revised and edited draft: It all has to come together in the best product or performance."

> *Don't feel compelled to use the same metaphors or anecdotes used by the English teacher. Find something comfortable for yourself.*

As you can see, metaphors and analogies work well to teach about concepts; perhaps you will find a metaphor that will help you talk with your students about the writing process. Don't feel compelled to use the same metaphors or anecdotes used by the English teacher. Find something comfortable for yourself. Using different stories with your students might "click" with some of them, unlike the stories and examples used by the English teacher. (As a former English teacher, I can vouch for the fact that teachers of other subjects often helped some of my students understand the writing process or note-taking better than I did—because they spoke from their own perspectives.)

Revising

After drafting, writers often engage in revision and editing before presenting the product to the intended audience, which is called "publishing." It is entirely appropriate for certain kinds of classroom writing to end at the drafting stage (for instance, a learning log entry). As noted earlier, some writing may even end at the prewriting stage, such as when students complete a graphic organizer or make a list. *When you assign writing, you must decide if the required evidence of learning will be a polished product or not.* Because learning logs and various forms of journals are meant to allow students to grapple with ideas, it's okay for their writing *not* to end up in a published form. These assignments are for writing-to-learn, and are highly metacognitive in nature; the point is not to publish for people other than oneself and the teacher. Writing that is intended to show mastery of content or to report on something specific, though, *must be* revised and edited and shaped into a product that clearly demonstrates the learning and the basics of the assigned written form.

Revision is the process of changing the writing so that it's the best it can be; therefore, much of the work of revision is about content, organization, and style. Students, however, can (and do) inadvertently get the idea that revision is mostly about correctness. *Editing* is about correctness. Make sure that your students know the difference!

> ### 〜 〜
> *Revision can consist of restarting, adding, deleting, and reorganizing what has already been drafted. It should be a highly creative part of the writing process.*

It was always helpful for me to discuss the word "revision" with my students by representing it this way: RE vision. This is how I've written the word on the board for my own students, in two parts, with the prefix exaggerated. The word's origins include the Latin *revisere*, which means "to look at again." Students should think of the act of revision as *seeing* the draft with new eyes—actually "revisioning" it; therefore, I teach them this meaning. I don't want them to get revision confused with the finer points of editing that become important just before publication.

Revision can consist of restarting, adding, deleting, and reorganizing what has already been drafted. It should be a highly creative part of the writing process. Donald Murray, an expert in writing instruction, has often said that writing *is* rewriting (1982). Many of us who write extensively for our jobs can also testify that revision is the part of the process that often yields the greatest results.

We should applaud and support our students' efforts in revising their work. The authors of *Write for College: A Student Handbook* remind us: "...Revision takes courage. It's easy to edit and proofread your writing and then turn it in. It's not so easy to improve the content of your writing—the thoughts, feelings, and details that carry your message—before submitting it. Revision is the important process of making changes in your writing until it says exactly what you want it to say" (Sebranek, Meyer, and Kemper 1997, p. 29). More good advice comes from teacher and author Laura Robb: "Let your writing cool. Put it away for a few days. Then start to revise." (http://content.scholastic.com/browse/article.jsp?id=4490). If we can allow for this "cooling off" process, we can help our students improve their written products tremendously.

In a content-area class other than language arts, it's hard to provide time for all that's needed to support writers. However, if you want a polished, final, written product, you must provide some time between the drafting and revising stages. Otherwise, students will not be giving you their best work, and their learning of content will not be enhanced as deeply. Increased time spent thinking about the topics of the writing leads to enhanced learning. Whatever you can do to extend the time between drafts is desirable.

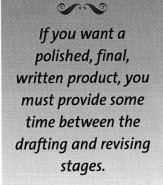

If you want a polished, final, written product, you must provide some time between the drafting and revising stages.

Editing

Editing is altogether different from revision. The focus of editing is on conventions of form or genre (for example, a poem looks different from an essay, and line breaks and indentations have special meaning); conventions of language (punctuation, capitalization, word usage, etc.); and conventions of publication (for instance, you generally do not use three different fonts and six-inch margins in a research paper). Editing is the stage of the writing process that many English instructors absolutely love, because it gives them a chance to exhibit their sophisticated understanding of conventions; ironically it's often the stage that students loathe, because they feel that they will never have enough knowledge to understand exactly what the teacher wants them to do. Students are quite nervous at this stage, because they may have experienced much editing criticism in their past.

Careful revision and editing are necessary components of any written product that demonstrates important content knowledge and the proficient execution of academic skills. If you have taught your students about the Revolutionary War for a few weeks, you don't want to assign a paper on some aspect of the war and then have students hurriedly scribble out only one draft in one class period. Ideally, you want an essay or research paper that presents a position or describes something related to the war in great detail, that offers compelling examples or evidence, that accurately cites any outside sources used, and that proves to you that the student has met the intended learning outcomes. You want to be able to pick up the paper and read it, following its logical organizational pattern and appreciating its accepted use of conventions. You also want the paper to sound like the student is sitting down with you to have a fairly formal conversation about his or her learning; the paper doesn't need to sound like an online encyclopedia or the textbook, but instead like the student, speaking in an academic tone.

This is the kind of polished writing that requires revision and editing, and perhaps you don't have to go it alone. If students have the good fortune of being in your class and have another teacher who is a specialist in English language arts, then you and that teacher should see if you can work together to assist the students. Also, focused revision and editing is a good idea. Kids can't "fix" everything at once in their writing. Ample research evidence suggests that concentrating on just a few weaknesses at a time builds competence, confidence, and excitement in writing. (You will read more about those ideas later in this book.)

Before tackling editing with your students—whether you are doing it alone or with the support of colleagues—you must study any writing rubrics related to your state standards and/or state testing. The criteria for good writing outlined in state rubrics will help you determine what conventions to emphasize to your students.

Publishing

Publication is the last step in the writing process. This stage generally refers to the time when writing is read or received by the intended audience, whether that audience is just the teacher, the teacher and classmates, or an audience that is wider than those who populate the writer's classroom.

Despite some common misconceptions, the publishing stage does not have to include elaborately decorated final drafts, hallway displays, oral presentations, or anything beyond your reading and responding to the papers, although there certainly may be times when you want to celebrate student writing. The most important step that you can take to keep writers thinking and growing is to read their work with careful attention and offer constructive feedback. Then the writing process can begin anew!

Written Reflections

1. When I began reading this chapter, did I have any misconceptions about the writing process, or any "fuzzy understandings"? If so, have I clarified my thinking? How?

_____

_____

_____

_____

_____

_____

_____

_____

2. What metaphor might I share with students to help them deepen their understanding of the writing process?

_____

_____

_____

_____

_____

_____

_____

3. What topic(s) do my students study that could lend themselves to a product that would go through the entire writing process?

_____

_____

_____

_____

_____

_____

_____

CHAPTER 3

Knowing Good Writing and Providing Effective Feedback

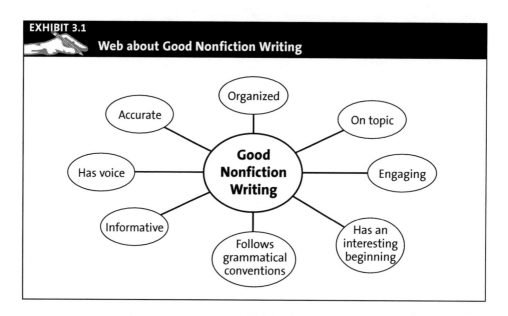

EXHIBIT 3.1

Web about Good Nonfiction Writing

Organized

Accurate

On topic

Has voice

Good Nonfiction Writing

Engaging

Informative

Follows grammatical conventions

Has an interesting beginning

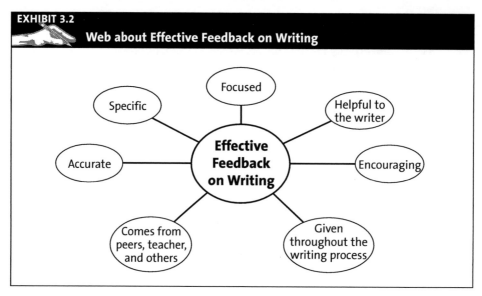

EXHIBIT 3.2

Web about Effective Feedback on Writing

Focused

Specific

Helpful to the writer

Accurate

Effective Feedback on Writing

Encouraging

Comes from peers, teacher, and others

Given throughout the writing process

Even teachers who have taught writing for years might disagree on some of the finer points about what "good writing" actually is. However, in order for any teacher to discuss effective writing with students and give them quality feedback on their written products, some common language must be adopted.

This chapter will help you solidify your understanding of effective writing, analyze what various documents say about student writing, and provide constructive feedback to your students.

The Components of Effective Nonfiction Writing

What's the most recent "good" piece of writing that you've read? For me, it was a recent article in *Education Week*. I was drowsily awaiting takeoff in Atlanta and pulled the periodical out of my bag. As I thumbed through it, I read several articles, with music from my iPod blasting in my ears. However, when I started reading this piece, I switched the music off before I hit the fourth paragraph. I said to myself, "I need to pay closer attention to this article. It's powerful!" I knew I had to give it my undivided attention in order to really absorb all the details.

We must help our students understand the qualities of effective nonfiction writing, and in order to do that, we must help them recognize it and articulate specifics about it.

I'm sure you've experienced similar reactions to a bold editorial, a compelling speech, or a finely crafted historical account. Good nonfiction writing is good writing, period—and it's good for many reasons. Nonetheless, certain qualities are paramount: rich, relevant content; an effective organizational pattern; the proper use of English language conventions; and a sense of who is "behind the words"—distinctive stylistic devices or a unique voice. The article I read that day on the plane certainly had all of these characteristics, and it was indeed an exemplary essay.

We must help our students understand the qualities of effective nonfiction writing, and in order to do that, we must help them recognize it and articulate specifics about it. So let's discuss each of the components of good nonfiction writing briefly. Again, it may be helpful for you to keep in mind an exemplary essay, editorial, or speech that you've read recently.

Content is simply the ideas presented in any piece of writing. Content includes the main points plus the supporting details, evidence, and examples. Content is basically *what* the writer says more than *how* he or she says it.

Sometimes content is called "ideas" or the "topic." These words are used more often in elementary school, however. Help your students understand that the words "content," "ideas," and "topic" may be synonymous in some teachers' minds, and help them understand that they all refer to the thoughts of the writer that appear in the paper.

> ✑〰
>
> *Proper use of conventions helps us communicate clearly. We should help our students become strong in conventions so they avoid surface errors that can detract seriously from content.*

Organization is *how* the writing is put together. A lab report in science class is structured quite differently from a literary analysis essay in English class. An article in the local newspaper is structured quite differently from that book-length biography of a historical figure that you might peruse in bed at night. All writing, in order to be understood, must have a clear organizational structure, and there are many such structures, from the very general and broad (paragraphs versus bulleted lists) to the highly specific (a spatial essay pattern describing a place first from left to right and then from top to bottom).

Conventions are all about *how* a writer says something. You could not be reading this book if I were not following certain conventions of the English language, like using properly punctuated, complete sentences. If I were not indenting my paragraphs or spelling my words correctly, my message would be garbled. Conventions include grammar, syntax, mechanics, and usage, although most people refer to conventions simply as "grammar." A good way to understand conventions is to remember that "writing that is strong in conventions has been proofread and edited with care" (http://www.nwrel.org/assessment/scoring.php?odelay= 3&d=1&r=6#definition). Proper use of conventions helps us communicate clearly. We should help our students become strong in conventions so they avoid surface errors that can detract seriously from content.

Style is perhaps the hardest quality of writing to discuss because it can't be easily quantified. It does, however, become clear through examples. Here is one: You would never confuse Charles Dickens and John Grisham. Granted, they are novelists and not primarily writers of nonfiction, but you probably get the point. Let's turn our attention to nonfiction writers in mainstream media. *Newsweek* columnists George Will and Anna Quindlen are not easily confused; neither are popular syndicated newspaper columnists Dave Barry (a humorist) and Leonard Pitts (more of a social commentator). The news reporting styles of Dan Rather and Katie Couric are quite different, as are the public speaking styles of the reverends Jesse Jackson and Billy Graham. Once an audience is familiar with a writer's style, it's hard to confuse that person with another writer. Students, too, can develop their unique styles, even with all forms of academic, nonfiction writing, and you, as their teacher, can help them in this endeavor—plus enjoy their writing as they become increasingly competent and distinct.

One handbook for secondary teachers includes a fitting discussion of style. This guide says that style "is the control of language that is appropriate to the purpose, audience, and context of the writing task" (North Carolina Public Schools Writing Across the Curriculum *High School Teacher's Handbook* (accessed online 2008). This is a good, basic definition to commit to memory and to share with students.

In order for us to better understand style, we must focus on the smaller units of the composition: the sentences and the words. Style is partly about selecting the best words possible. In South Carolina, the state writing test rubric references "vivid vocabulary" (http://ed.sc.gov/agency/offices/assessment/PACT/ERrubric032204.doc). Vivid vocabulary is so much nicer than its opposite, which I assume would be "dull and boring vocabulary." Word choice is another important part of style, no matter how your particular writing rubric(s) or standards describe it (but do be on the lookout for the exact language used by the official documents of your state).

> *Students, too, can develop their unique styles, even with all forms of academic, nonfiction writing, and you, as their teacher, can help them in this endeavor—plus enjoy their writing as they become increasingly competent and distinct.*

The other key component of style is sentence structure. A variety of lengths and styles is preferable; who wants to read a series of sentences that all begin similarly and have the same basic structure and length? Some states, like Georgia, specifically demand in their academic standards that students write compound, complex, and compound-complex sentences. Even first-graders can learn, particularly through studying professional models, how to create varied sentences; don't hesitate to address sentence variety, if applicable, with your students.

Much about style can be taught best through the use of good models that you would like your students to emulate. In an advanced high school science class, for example, you would probably want an academic and somewhat detached style; surely the students should not be sprinkling the writing with flowery phrases or abundant adjectives that do nothing to further illuminate the scientific concepts being written about. Depending on the kinds of writing they are doing in such a class, however, models from *Popular Science* or *Scientific American* magazines might be appropriate. In another part of the school, a student in a child development class may be working on an explanation of a scientific phenomenon like the development of a rainbow or how a tadpole turns into a frog. In this case, you would not want to provide a writing model from a scientific magazine or journal. This student's audience would be young children; therefore, the writing would need to use an appropriate style for that particular age group. You could perhaps share style examples from children's books or parents' magazines in this case.

Teachers who are charged primarily with teaching content—secondary teachers of science, math, history, music, art, health, technical education, and so on—have very limited time to discuss the particulars of style with students. However, a few strong examples can go a long way.

Why Worry About Good Writing in Content-Area Classes?

Let's look at some ways in which professional educational organizations discuss good writing. You may be a member of one or more of these organizations, but even if you aren't, you'll probably appreciate what they have to say about writing and its connection to learning in all of the disciplines. You also may get ideas about how to discuss good writing more thoroughly with students, especially as good writing relates specifically to your content area.

The National Council of Teachers of English (NCTE) obviously has a great deal to say about teaching writing, and some of its strongest statements are about writing across the curriculum. The NCTE urges teachers of all subjects to use writing, saying that it is "integral in every subject" (http://www.ncte.org/edpolicy/writing/research/122398.htm). One of the NCTE's core principles is that writing is a tool for thinking and is necessary for effective teaching (http://www.ncte.org/edpolicy/writing/about/122369.htm). The necessity of having students write in order for them to deepen their own learning is a core premise of this book and is supported strongly by the NCTE.

Professional groups in other subject areas concur with the NCTE's positions. The National Council of Teachers of Mathematics (NCTM) urges teachers to teach students how to align factual knowledge and procedural proficiency with conceptual knowledge and mentions that students must "recognize the importance of reflecting on their thinking" (http://www.nctm.org/standards/12752_exec_pssm.pdf). Writing about your learning—what was hard, what was confusing, what was easy—is an excellent way to learn more about mathematical concepts. Obviously, the student with a deeper understanding of math concepts will be far more successful on all standardized measures of math achievement and will do well on classroom assessments. Math teachers should incorporate reflective thinking and writing activities in order to deepen their students' math understanding.

The NCTM Process Standards note, "When students are challenged to communicate the results of their thinking to others orally or in writing, they learn to be clear, convincing, and precise in their use of mathematical language" (http://www.nctm.org/standards/12752_exec_pssm.pdf). Communicating in words, whether it is done in writing or orally, assists students with mathematical language and supports their increasingly sophisticated use of specific math vocabulary.

> *Writing about your learning—what was hard, what was confusing, what was easy—is an excellent way to learn more about mathematical concepts.*

NCTM cautions that "explanations should include mathematical arguments and rationales, not just procedural descriptions or summaries" (http://www.nctm.org/standards/12752_exec_pssm.pdf). While descriptive writing that outlines procedures and written summaries are both useful assignments to do in the mathematics classroom, this statement highlights the critical thinking and persuasive writing that students should do in all of their classes. We want them to be able to make justifiable arguments and to have well-supported rationales for any content they are studying. It's up to us as their teachers to guide them in these forms of communication.

The National Science Teachers Association (NSTA) specifically refers to "performance assessment," "portfolio construction," "problem-based learning scenarios," and "writing challenges" in its position statement on assessment (http://www.nsta.org/positionstatement&psid=40). The statement goes on to say that quality science assessments must collect information on students' abilities to think critically. It's difficult to assess critical thinking without having students write or explain aloud. As a teacher, I unfortunately don't have the time for an extended conversation with each student every day or even once a week. If I could, then I might ask probing questions to stimulate critical thinking so that I could gauge each student's level of understanding. Therefore, having students respond to content-based writing prompts makes a lot of sense. I can read those responses and get a good feel for who's catching on, who's ready to move on, and who needs additional assistance in order to be ready for what's coming next.

The College Board, makers of the SAT, added a writing component in 2005. Its Web site claims that this change was made in part to meet the changing needs of students, teachers, and college admissions staff. The College Board asserts that the addition of writing to the test will strengthen its predictive validity and help colleges to make better admissions decisions. It is also noted that the addition of writing should "reinforce the importance of writing skills throughout a student's education and support the improvement of the academic preparation of all students, bolstering their chances for academic success in college" (http://www.collegeboard.com/highered/ra/sat/sat_faqs.html#quest3). Many educators are concerned that the twenty-five-minute period for students to complete the essay is insufficient; the NCTE is chief among the organizations protesting (see http://www.ncte.org/library/files/About_NCTE/Press_Center/SAT/SAT-ACT-tf-report.pdf). However, the addition of the writing component to the SAT at least brings writing to the attention of secondary teaches like no other measure could.

Just What Should You Grade?

If your students have produced good writing, then you must provide feedback on it. Many times, that feedback includes a grade of some sort. First, realize that *not all writing assignments need to be graded*. This is especially important for content-area teachers, because thinking about grading every piece of writing often hinders teachers from assigning enough writing tasks. Second, embrace the notion that you can give considerable feedback to students about writing *without* giving them a grade. These two core ideas are essential to creating a healthy writing environment in any academic class.

The personalized attention that a teacher provides when working with a student one-on-one or in a small group is often what students remember far longer than they remember a grade scrawled on a sheet of paper or all of those red circles.

Feedback about the content of the writing can be given to students throughout the writing process. The personalized attention that a teacher provides when working with a student one-on-one or in a small group is often what students remember far longer than they remember a grade scrawled on a sheet of paper or all of those red circles. Also, writing brief comments on students' papers during the drafting and revising phases is appreciated by students and can be very useful, especially if the comments focus on what the writer is doing well and on genuine questions that you have as a reader.

Evaluation, which ideally employs a rubric clearly delineating several perform-ance levels, is necessary when students complete the writing process and give you a publication-quality draft (meaning that it is suitable for, at a minimum, the teacher and the classmates). Other writing assignments that are more formative in nature must be evaluated using a different rubric.

How Should You Grade Writing?

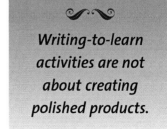

Writing-to-learn activities are not about creating polished products.

Let's return to the core idea of not grading everything. Don't "grade" writing-to-learn assignments. Consider giving some kind of effort or completion score if your school's grading system allows for it (or if you feel that students won't com-plete the work otherwise), but remember that writing-to-learn activities are not about creating polished products. They are for the writer's benefit; they are meant to encourage deeper understanding within the mind of the learner. They are also useful for the teacher. By reading and providing even infor-mal feedback on these assignments, you can "ratchet up" the quality of instruction because you have a better understanding of student learning. Writing does "dou-ble duty": It has a cognitive effect that enhances student learning, and it helps the teacher to tailor instruction immediately to student needs.

Mondschein-Leist (1997) suggests that writing-to-learn assignments can be used to stimulate discussion, monitor overall understanding of a class, provide review for the students, or reinforce the learning of information that students have not mastered.

Therefore, when you create a writing assignment, you must first consider your *purpose*. Do you want to see how students are learning—where they stand or how they're doing in the current unit? If so, you are going to assign a *writing-to-learn* activity, like a learning log entry, an exit slip, or an impromptu composition, prob-ably written in only one sitting and in only one draft. The purpose is for the stu-dent to grapple with course content, and any feedback or grading must be focused on that primary purpose. A system of checks, pluses, and minuses always worked well for me, and many teachers find it easy to implement. (See Exhibit 3.3, which provides three examples using this format.)

Some teachers have wonderful ways to discuss levels of performance with stu-dents. For example, one teacher tells her students that the plus level of the rubric "has the wow factor." The check level "gets the job done," and the minus level "doesn't do the trick." She spends time when first using the rubric to show exam-

EXHIBIT 3.3

Examples of Rubrics for Writing-to-Learn

Rubric A

This writing-to-learn rubric provides a quick score to each student and is only for completion of the task.

+	✔	−	No score or redo
The response demonstrates all of the qualities for ✔ and also includes unique insight or an extraordinary example.	The response is on topic and is of an appropriate length to demonstrate understanding of the targeted content, concept(s), or skill(s).	The response is partially off topic or is insufficient in length to demonstrate understanding of the targeted content, concept(s), or skill(s).	The response is illegible, entirely off-topic, or the student did not do a response.

Rubric B

This writing-to-learn rubric provides a score to all students and gives recognition with specific feedback to students who write an advanced response.

+	✔	−	No score or redo
The response demonstrates all of the qualities for ✔ and also includes this unique insight or extraordinary example.	The response is on topic and is of an appropriate length to demonstrate understanding of the targeted content, concept(s), or skill(s).	The response is partially off topic or is insufficient in length to demonstrate understanding of the targeted content, concept(s), or skill(s).	The response is illegible or entirely off-topic, or the student did not do a response.
_____ _____ _____ _____ _____			

ples from each level. Another teacher told me that she tells her students that if they score proficient (check), they "leapt over the tall building." The exemplary (plus) level means that the student "cleared the building with room to spare." However, the minus level means that the student "smashed into the building but at least

EXHIBIT 3.3

Examples of Rubrics for Writing-to-Learn *(continued)*

Rubric C

This writing-to-learn rubric provides specific feedback to students who write an advanced response and to those nearing proficiency.

+	✔	−	No score or redo
The response demonstrates all of the qualities for ✔ and also includes this unique insight or extraordinary example.	The response is on topic and is of an appropriate length to demonstrate understanding of the targeted content, concept(s), or skill(s).	The response is partially off topic or is insufficient in length to demonstrate understanding of the targeted content, concept(s), or skill(s). Next time try this:	The response is illegible or entirely off-topic, or the student did not do a response.
_____ _____ _____ _____ _____		_____ _____ _____	

tried." If the student doesn't get a score, it means "his or her feet stayed on the ground." The last comparison I'll share is based on Oreo cookies: A check is just an Oreo. The plus level is a double-stuffed, chocolate-coated Oreo, and the minus level is the Oreo with the filling removed. No score is called "smashed-up Oreo cookie crumbs with no filling." Find a metaphor that works for you and your rubric, or use one of these to get started.

Sometimes a simple rubric of check, plus, and minus won't work. If your purpose is to have students demonstrate understanding of or proficiency in required content, you *must* provide feedback and score differently. It's best to have a rubric delineating four levels of proficiency demonstrated in the final written product: exemplary/advanced, proficient, nearly proficient or progressing, and not yet near proficient. Each level needs specific criteria to make clear to students exactly what is expected. Some teachers find that having only three levels works well first: the exemplary, proficient, and nearly proficient levels. As you become more "tuned in" to specific problems faced by the struggling students, the bottom level may begin to "split," and you may revise the rubric to show what the difference really is

EXHIBIT 3.4

Content-Area Rubrics

1. Middle School Science

Trait	4	3	2	1
Ideas	• The writing is focused on one clearly identified main idea (the rock cycle). • The main idea is supported by relevant supporting details about the rock cycle, including the following in addition to what is specified in score point 3: _____ _____ _____	• The writing is focused on one main idea (the rock cycle). • The main idea is supported by supporting details (about igneous, metamorphic, and sedimentary rock).	• The writing has an attempt at a main idea. • More supporting details are needed.	• A main idea cannot be identified. • Details are absent.
Organization	• The writing has a clear beginning, middle, and end, appropriate for the writing task (expository essay). • Details are presented in an interesting and logical order.	• The writing has a clear beginning, middle, and end. • Details are presented in a logical order.	• The writing is missing a clear beginning, middle, or end, or is missing more than one of these parts. • Details are presented in a disorganized way.	• The writing has no clear organizational plan.
Conventions	• The writing has no errors in capitalization of first words of sentences or in end marks (periods, exclamation points, question marks). • The writing is free of unintentional fragments and run-ons.	• The writing may have minimal errors in initial capitalization or end marks, but these do not detract from the overall meaning. • The writing may have minimal fragments and run-ons, but these do not detract from the overall meaning.	• The writing has several serious errors in initial capitalization and end marks. • The writing has several fragments and run-ons that detract from the overall meaning.	• The writing has many serious errors in initial capitalization and end marks. • The writing has many fragments and run-ons.

EXHIBIT 3.4

Content-Area Rubrics (continued)

2. Middle School Social Studies

	4	3	2	1
Ideas (Content)*	• Demonstrates all the qualities of a level 3 response and includes an analysis of the significance of the siege of Savannah	• General focus on topic (Georgia's involvement in the American Revolution) • Developed controlling idea • Sufficient details, including a discussion of the views of Loyalists and patriots and a correct sequence of main events	• Limited focus on topic • Attempted controlling idea • Limited details	• Lack of focus on topic • Lack of controlling idea • Lack of details
Organization	• Clearly defined introduction, body, and conclusion paragraphs • Logical and appropriate sequence of ideas • Effective and varied use of transitions	• Presents introduction, body, and conclusion paragraphs • Has clear sequence of ideas • Effective use of transitions	• Lacks either an introduction OR conclusion paragraph • Unclear sequence of ideas • Ineffective use of transitions	• Lacks introduction AND conclusion paragraphs • Lack of sequencing • Lack of transitions
Conventions	• All paragraphing is correct • Simple, compound, and complex sentences are present and have correct end punctuation • No errors in sentence formation (no unintentional fragments; no run-ons)	• Paragraphing is generally correct • Simple, compound, and complex sentences are present and have correct end punctuation • Some errors in sentence formation may be present but do not detract from the overall meaning	• Paragraphing is attempted • Simple sentences are present and are generally correct; other sentence types may have errors • Occasional fragments and run-ons detract from overall meaning	• Control of paragraphing is not evident • Overall, sentence structure is awkward, and end punctuation is frequently incorrect or missing

*Content is weighted twice as much as the other domains.

between a student who is close to proficiency and one who is further away. (Refer to Exhibit 3.4 for examples using science and social studies.)

When designing an initial rubric, in many cases you can take the general writing rubric for your state and "layer in" your content requirements in the ideas/content section. This may be the section of the rubric that you would weight most heavily when determining a final score or letter grade. However, you will probably also want to address, at minimum, the organization of the writing. Organization of writing is critical in all subject areas and changes dramatically only for specialized forms of writing, like a lab report.

Initially, you may want to address only very limited considerations in style and conventions. As you become more comfortable with using writing in your classes, you will naturally adapt your rubrics so that they work better each time. You may also come to agreements with other members of your faculty about common expectations for organization and conventions; many schools that have used common rubrics find certain areas upon which everyone can agree. For example, sentence fragments and run-on sentences are never okay—not in any class, not in any piece of revised writing. Once a convention like this is emphasized schoolwide, students get the message that clear communication and good writing are important everywhere—not just in English class.

Keep in mind that your main goal for using writing is to enhance each student's content-area learning.

Keep in mind that your main goal for using writing is to enhance each student's content-area learning. You will need to find methods for providing feedback on and grading writing that allow you to be both effective and efficient. Spending hours of your own time marking errors or writing copious comments will not help your students learn the content better; instead, *you* will be learning it better yourself, along with sharpening your own grammatical skills. The *students* are the ones who need to write, rewrite, and become more expert in content, *not you!* Keep this point in mind as you plan for providing feedback on their writing.

What Do State Standards Say About Good Writing?

State writing rubrics are remarkably similar in how they discuss the qualities of effective writing. Let's look at some examples and discuss how we might approach these ideas with our students and possibly build scoring guides to use in our own classes based on the ideas. We're going to use a modified "unwrapping" process (Ainsworth 2003), applied to a rubric instead of to standards in this case.

In New York, the top level of writing performance (which exceeds the state standard) in grade eight includes the following:

> Taken as a whole, the responses fulfill the requirements of the tasks … develop ideas fully with thorough elaboration; make effective use of relevant and accurate examples … In addition, the extended response establishes and maintains a clear focus; shows a logical sequence of ideas through the use of appropriate transitions or other devices; is fluent and easy to read, with a sense of engagement or voice; uses varied sentence structure and some above-grade-level vocabulary (New York State Education Department, information booklet for scoring the Regents comprehensive examination in English; available online at http://www.emsc.nysed.gov/osa/hsgen/det541e-608.pdf; accessed 2008).

This particular writing rubric is holistic, meaning that all of the indicators are "lumped" together and a score is given. This rubric is also intended to be used with a text that students read and to which they write a response; I have omitted some of the text-specific references. Many times on state writing tests, though, students will be writing only to a prompt and will not read a text first.

The New York components should sound familiar to you if you read the previous chapter. You should clearly see content, organization, and style.

Let's "unwrap" this portion of the scoring guide and represent it in the three categories it appears to contain: content, organization, and style. In Exhibit 3.5 you will see the words and phrases from the holistic rubric now represented in analytic style.

EXHIBIT 3.5
"Unwrapped" Information from New York Rubric

Content	Organization	Style
Requirements of the task	Sequence	Fluent
Ideas	Transitions	Easy to read
Elaboration		Engagement
Examples		Voice
Focus		Varied sentence structure
		Vocabulary

Don't be fooled by the bulk of information in the style column. Regardless of the parameters of any writing assignment, a couple of items are of utmost importance, and you see them here: The question must be answered or the prompt addressed ("fulfill the requirements of the task"), and details must be provided ("develop ideas fully with thorough elaboration"). The first two columns represent the most crucial aspects of the writing, and these qualities (content and organization) would be a good starting point for building a writing rubric for any content-area class.

First and foremost, students need to analyze any writing prompt or question asked, then they need to plan the details that they will provide. Style (a sense of engagement or voice, varied sentence structure, and vocabulary) is usually secondary to these concerns. The New York holistic rubric does not address conventions. Many states even have separate scoring guides for conventions. That's another idea you could adapt for your classroom. For instance, create a rubric in which content and organization together are weighted as two-thirds or three-fourths of the grade, and in which conventions makes up the rest of the total.

Rubrics from the state of Washington assess content, organization, and style together in one rubric and conventions separately. The grade 10 exemplary level in Washington for content, organization, and style includes the following descriptors:

- Maintains consistent focus on topic and has selected and relevant details

- Has a logical organizational pattern and conveys a sense of completeness and wholeness

- Provides transitions which clearly serve to connect ideas

- Uses language effectively by exhibiting word choices that are engaging and appropriate for intended audience and purpose

EXHIBIT 3.6

Draft 1 of an Analytic Rubric from Washington

Content	Organization
• Has a consistent focus on the assigned topic • Has relevant details	• Has a logical organizational pattern • Conveys a sense of wholeness • Uses transitions

- Includes sentences, or phrases where appropriate, of varied length and structure
- Allows the reader to sense the person behind the words (Washington Office of Superintendent of Public Instruction; writing assessment available online at http://www.k12.wa.us/assessment/WASL/Writing/resources.aspx).

Staying on topic, as dictated by the question or prompt, is once again very important. The development of the writing in terms of details is also critical. A "logical organizational pattern" must exist, and transitions are specifically mentioned, as they are in the New York rubric. Word choice, which is another way to say vocabulary, appears here. Varied phrase/sentence structure is noted, and the "voice" of the piece ("the person behind the words") is mentioned last. Again, for the writer, it all boils down to staying on topic, using strong details, providing transitions, displaying appropriate use of vocabulary, varying sentence structures and lengths, and being somewhat original so that the paper doesn't sound like all of the other papers. For the teacher, teaching about organizational patterns, transitions, and vocabulary are important in helping student writers be the best that they can be.

If I were a Washington teacher, I could start with a classroom writing rubric similar to what is displayed in Exhibit 3.6.

If I wanted to include style, my initial draft of the qualities of proficient writing might look like the rubric shown in Exhibit 3.7.

EXHIBIT 3.7 Draft 2 of an Analytic Rubric from Washington		
Content	**Organization**	**Style**
• Has a consistent focus on the assigned topic • Has relevant details	• Has a logical organizational pattern • Conveys a sense of wholeness • Uses transitions	• Uses engaging and appropriate word choices • Varies sentence length and structure • Allows the reader to sense the person behind the words

You'll see that the Washington rubric does not include conventions, but I could add some in my own draft, again at the proficient level (see Exhibit 3.8).

EXHIBIT 3.8

Draft 3 of an Analytic Rubric from Washington

Content	Organization	Style	Conventions
• Has a consistent focus on the assigned topic • Has relevant details	• Has a logical organizational pattern • Conveys a sense of wholeness • Uses transitions	• Uses engaging and appropriate word choices • Varies sentence length and structure • Allows the reader to sense the person behind the words	• Is written in the assigned form (essay, lab report, research report, etc.) • Content-area terminology is used correctly and is spelled correctly • Any errors in grammar, mechanics, and usage do not seriously detract from the overall meaning

> *Content and organization are generally the first two areas that students must grasp well in order for their subject-area writing to be proficient; increasing sophistication in style and conventions comes later.*

In order to create the exemplary level, I would have to ask myself how I could change the indicators in Exhibits 3.6 through 3.8 both qualitatively and quantitatively to more clearly specify excellence as opposed to proficiency.

Again, just because the style and conventions columns have more detail than the content and organization columns *does not mean* that they are more important. Content and organization are generally the first two areas that students must grasp well in order for their subject-area writing to be proficient; increasing sophistication in style and conventions comes later.

The Florida rubric for eighth grade has a somewhat different way of describing its writing requirements. Conventions are addressed in this holistic rubric only in the last sentence. This description represents what an exemplary response would do:

> The writing is focused, purposeful, and reflects insight into the writing situation. The paper conveys a sense of completeness and wholeness with adherence to the main idea, and its organizational

pattern provides for a logical progression of ideas. The support is substantial, specific, relevant, concrete, and/or illustrative. The paper demonstrates a commitment to and an involvement with the subject, clarity in presentation of ideas, and may use creative writing strategies appropriate to the purpose of the paper. The writing demonstrates a mature command of language (word choice) with freshness of expression. Sentence structure is varied, and sentences are complete except when fragments are used purposefully. Few, if any, convention errors occur in mechanics, usage, and punctuation (Florida Department of Education, FCAT writing rubric grade 8; available online at http://fcat.fldoe.org/pdf/rubrcw08.pdf).

Notice that even a paper that receives the highest score in a testing situation is never described as being free of errors in conventions. The phrase "few, if any" is quite useful in this regard.

Let's analyze some other parts of the Florida description of exemplary writing. Cohesion is specifically addressed ("a sense of completeness and wholeness"). The writing is not dry and perfunctory, merely reporting facts or walking through common examples, because the paper "demonstrates a commitment to and an involvement with the subject." Much of the writing that students do in school is dry, dull, and lifeless, much like an encyclopedia entry. This part of the description would let teachers know that they must help students find engaging ways to write about their subjects, and in so doing, they would probably have to utilize models of writing that do just that.

"Vivid vocabulary," a phrase that was mentioned earlier from the South Carolina writing rubric, shows up in Florida's version as "freshness of expression." Both of these phrases mean that the student writer chooses the best words possible. Varied sentence structure also appears in Florida's rubric, as it does in the scoring guides of many states. Thus, it can be inferred that helping students write sentences of different syntactical structures is important, as is helping them vary the length of their sentences for maximum impact.

Florida's language for a writing rubric is more like what students would hear in the English language arts classroom. Exhibit 3.9 shows how you might adapt the Florida rubric for a content area other than English language arts. This rubric describes exemplary writing.

In Exhibit 3.9, I took a large chunk of text and made it into ten bullets that represent the highest level of achievement in academic writing in my class.

EXHIBIT 3.9

Description of Exemplary Writing from Florida

Content	Organization	Style	Conventions
• Addresses the writing situation • Focuses on a main idea • Has substantial support (examples, details)	• Is complete, whole, and clear. • Has an organizational pattern that shows a logical progression of ideas	• May use appropriate creative writing strategies • Demonstrates a command of language (word choice) • Has varied sentence structure throughout	• Has complete and correct sentences (no unintentional fragments) • Has few, if any, errors in mechanics, punctuation, and/or usage

For the proficient level of that same rubric, I might use criteria similar to what is displayed in Exhibit 3.10.

Notice in Exhibit 3.10 how each indicator (bullet point) specifies achievement below the level of exemplary performance but also makes clear the expectation for meeting the standard. The two top levels of this rubric are not perfect, but they could be good starting points for my class as we tackle increased nonfiction writing.

The state of Virginia is well known for its Standards of Learning. Its eighth grade holistic rubric for written expression is described in the following quotation. At the highest score point:

> "The writer demonstrates consistent, though not necessarily perfect, control of the written expression domain's features. The result is a purposefully crafted message that the reader remembers, primarily because its precise information and vocabulary resonate as images in the reader's mind. Highly specific word choice and information also create tone in the writing and enhance the writer's voice ... The writer repeats or varies sentence construction for effect and appropriately subordinates ideas and embeds modifiers on a regular basis, resulting in a rhythmic flow throughout the piece (Virginia Department of Education, Virginia standards of learning assessments; blueprint grade 8 writing test; available online at http://www.doe.virginia.gov/VDOE/Assessment/EnglishBlueprint05/BlueprintsG8writing.pdf).

EXHIBIT 3.10

Description of Proficient Writing from Florida

Content	Organization	Style	Conventions
• Addresses the writing situation • Focuses on a main idea but may go off topic in an instance or two • Has adequate support (examples, details)	• Is complete • Has an organizational pattern that shows a logical progression of ideas	• Uses appropriate writing strategies • Has effective word choice • Has one or two examples of varied sentence structure	• Has mostly complete sentences; may have one or two unintentional fragments • Has few errors in mechanics, punctuation, and/or usage

This is perhaps the most specific we've seen so far in terms of how the writing is described based on its features. Let's "unwrap" that standard now for content, organization, style, and conventions.

Conventions, as far as the rules for writing in any given form, are referred to at the beginning: "control of the . . . domain's features." This means that if the student is asked to write a letter or an editorial, then the writing doesn't take the form of a poem or song. However, it doesn't mean that the command of the assigned form is perfect, even at this exemplary level. Therefore, if the required form is a letter, the student would have to have the basics of letter form: probably a heading, salutation, body, closing, and signature. However, if the student left off the heading, which consists of the date and the address from which the letter is being sent, this omission may not prevent the student from getting the highest score point as long as the rest of the parts were obvious and the other criteria were met.

The Virginia rubric is the only one we have seen thus far specifying imagery ("images in the reader's mind"). Imagery is not always appropriate in content areas other than English language arts; therefore, this particular component could probably be omitted.

Content must include "precise information," and style consists of word choice as well as tone, or the attitude evident toward the subject being addressed. Again, a variety of sentence structures is desirable ("varies sentence construction for effect"). Being able to use subordinate ideas is specified; this would indicate that teachers need to show students how to use various forms of phrases and clauses in their writing to combine ideas. The embedded modifiers mentioned in the rubric

EXHIBIT 3.11

Description of Proficient Writing from Virginia

Content	Organization	Style	Conventions
• Contains both general and specific information related to the assigned topic • Has a clear message	• Creates a sense of "flow" through logical organization of ideas, including a clear beginning, middle, and end	• Uses specific words • Creates a sense of "flow" through the use of varied sentence structures	• Is written in the assigned form • Has few errors in mechanics, punctuation, and/or usage

could include single words, phrases, and clauses. Both organization and style are tied together at the end of this rubric, as "rhythmic flow" is mentioned. This also sounds very literary and more appropriate to the content of English language arts classes, but we can adapt it for our content-area rubric.

Exhibit 3.11 gives suggestions for how to create the proficient level of a rubric based on what the state of Virginia mandates.

Colorado's rubric for extended written responses for grades 4 through 10 specifies the following at its top level for content and organization:

> The writing meets all requirements of the prompt; stays fully focused on topic; includes relevant information; provides main ideas and specific, elaborated details that move beyond the obvious; includes an inviting introduction, logical arrangements of ideas, and satisfying conclusion; maintains a clear order with transitions between ideas (Colorado Department of Education, *CSAP scoring information: Links to writing rubrics*; available online at http://www.cde.state. co.us/cdeassess/documents/csap/csap_scoring.html#Writing).

This description makes very clear what is expected in content and organization and uses vocabulary that teachers can use repeatedly with their students so that everyone is aware of the expectations. It's important for students to understand what is required by any prompt or assignment they are given. This is also important for them in testing situations. This part of the Colorado rubric states very clearly that the writer must meet the requirements laid out first and foremost. If a writer stays "fully focused on topic," this means that there are no extraneous details or sentences that wander off-point. This is a skill that teachers often have to focus on with their students, especially younger or more inexperienced writers.

Wandering off-topic or losing focus is not desirable in any kind of nonfiction writing. We must remind our students to save the loose connections and subplots for the poetry and fiction that they may be writing in their English classes!

Details that "move beyond the obvious" are reminiscent of what, in Florida's rubric, are called "substantial, specific, relevant, concrete, and/or illustrative" (Colorado Department of Education, *CSAP scoring information: Links to writing rubrics*; available online at http://www.cde.state.co.us/cdeassess/documents/csap/csap_scoring.html#Writing). The writer does not just give a catalog of details or select the most obvious ones to use; instead, the writer must show insight.

An introduction and conclusion are mentioned by name in the Colorado rubric, which means that the correct answer is most likely always going to be an essay of some sort. It's important for us to help our students understand exactly what introductions and conclusions are. I've worked with middle school students over the years who thought (erroneously) that phrases along the lines of "Today I'm going to write about" or "Hello" could serve as effective introductions and that "The end" could be a conclusion. Not so! But somewhere along the line they had been taught that these kinds of constructions were acceptable. *Only vigorous, focused teaching by an entire faculty helps our students unlearn bad writing habits.*

> ✐·❧
> *Only vigorous, focused teaching by an entire faculty helps our students unlearn bad writing habits.*

Lastly, transitions are mentioned in the rubric, as they are in many state writing rubrics and state standards. It then follows that all teachers would help students know what transitions are and would require transitions to be used, both between sentences and between paragraphs.

To distill what we have learned from these representative state writing expectations, let's examine this list of what is most important to emphasize with students in all nonfiction writing:

1. In *content*, students must address the prompt or question given and include ample supporting details in a way that is appropriate for the specific purpose, form, and audience.

2. In *organization*, the writing must come together as a whole (cohesion), have a logical organizational pattern, and use transitions that move the reader from idea to idea.

3. In *style*, the writing should show excellence in word choice (vocabulary) and exhibit sentence variety.

4. In *conventions*, few, if any, errors are evident. Any errors that are present do not seriously detract from the meaning that the writer is trying to impart.

Content-area teachers with whom I've worked from all over the United States have "unwrapped" their state's writing rubrics, examined the standards documents for their states, and produced rubrics that work for them. Exhibit 3.4 (page 42) displays two of those rubrics (one for middle school science and one for middle school social studies). You can individually or collaboratively work through a similar process and find a rubric that will work for you and your students.

How Do You Begin Talking About Good Writing with Students?

If you are a teacher in a subject other than English language arts, it may feel daunting to discuss writing with your students. If you have not had them write extensively in your class before now, one of the easiest and least threatening ways to begin talking about writing is to bring in an effective piece of writing related to the topic they are studying. This can be anything: an article out of a magazine or newspaper, something from the Internet, or perhaps an excerpt from an educational publication designed for students or teachers.

For this exercise, it's probably best not to use material directly from a textbook, because some textbook writing is notoriously bad, and because students often immediately "shut down" when they are asked to look in their textbooks. Copy this piece of writing for each student, or display it on the overhead so that you can all read and talk about it together. Ask them to read it silently. Then read it aloud. Tell them that you think it's a good piece of writing and that you shared it with them not only because it's about ___ (the topic at hand) but also because you think that it's effective.

Then ask them to articulate some of the reasons why they think that a teacher would consider this piece of writing to be good. If they have a hard time with that question, get them started by saying something like, "The first sentence really caught my attention and made me want to read further," or anything else that is truly a reason why you picked the piece. After a few minutes of this give and take, work with your students to categorize the comments made as being related to content (ideas), organization, style, or conventions. That may be enough for this particular mini-lesson on writing as part of your content area.

On a subsequent day, you can bring in another piece of writing, and again, work together to make and categorize comments about the writing. Of course, you want to discuss the subject-area content, too, but spend a few minutes focusing on the writing. You can then add to the collaborative class list of what makes for effective content, organization, style, and/or conventions. This collaborative list can become the basis for a rubric that you will later use when you ask students to write in your content-area class.

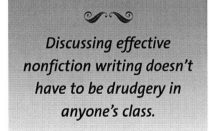

Discussing effective nonfiction writing doesn't have to be drudgery in anyone's class.

Another low-stress way to discuss the qualities of effective writing is to take an excerpt from a particularly dry section of your textbook or from an encyclopedia and ask the students to articulate the qualities of effectiveness. Because they have had previous practice with better examples, they may find themselves stumped and pretty quiet when you pose the question. Take the time to discuss what's not effective instead. You could even allow them to suggest revisions or to work in pairs and rewrite the excerpt, making it have more of the qualities that you have all agreed are important. This kind of activity readies your students for work later in revision and peer editing.

Discussing effective nonfiction writing doesn't have to be drudgery in anyone's class. Beginning with writing that you find powerful—and ideally, writing that connects somehow to your subject area—is a way for both you and your students to undertake the journey toward becoming better writers yourselves and toward sharing a language about the qualities of effective writing.

How Do You Give Kids Feedback About Their Writing?

Remember that if you have assigned a true "writing-to-learn" task, the only feedback that you may want to give is informal and directed at the entire class. You can walk around as students are writing to read over their shoulders, or you can collect the writing, or you can read it the next day as they open their notebooks and copy some introductory notes from the board—but remember, you do not have to "grade" the writing.

Allow me to illustrate with an example from my own teaching experience. I often taught ninth grade English, and in the two states in which I did this, I was required to teach a unit on Shakespeare in general and the play *Romeo and Juliet* in particular. For many years, I conducted an introductory lecture on Shakespeare's life and his writing. If I were to teach a similar lesson tomorrow, at the end of class, I could ask the students to write an exit slip of some sort. I could ask them what they remembered about Shakespeare from my lecture, and I could also ask for any questions they had and/or anything they wondered about one of the world's most famous writers.

That particular kind of writing assignment is designed to force my students to mull over the ideas I have presented, plus think about what else might be important. I would collect these responses and read them quickly, looking for any key misconceptions or intriguing questions, perhaps entering a quick mark in the gradebook for each student who completed the assignment. The next day, I could

---

EXHIBIT 3.12

Peer Response Sheets

Writer's name: _____

As the writer of this piece, I would like help with _____

_____

Listener's name: _____

As the listener for this writer, I share these comments: _____

_____

One thing that I liked or that stood out to me was _____

_____

One question I have is _____

_____

I suggest you _____

_____

The writer decides what to do next. Doing nothing is NOT an option!

open class with general comments about the content of the exit slips. In this way, I would be providing each class with general feedback about their comments, and they could see that their teacher was acting upon their ideas.

Writing assignments that go through multiple drafts deserve more personalized and more specific feedback, obviously. Remember that feedback on rough drafts does not have to come from you; peer response processes, if orchestrated well, can provide students with much helpful feedback. Indeed, a recent meta-analysis by Graham and Perin (2007) shows an effect size of 0.75 for peer response on writing, and as the authors note, "These investigations show that collaborative arrangements where students help each other with one or more aspects of their writing had a strong and positive impact on writing quality." Sample peer response sheets (Exhibit 3.12) are included in this chapter and may be suitable for adaptation in your classes. Some teachers require students to have two or three peer conferences prior to submitting a draft for teacher feedback.

Another caution: Resist the urge to use profuse written commentary or to mark all of the grammatical errors you find, especially once a draft has been submitted for a final grade. The meta-analysis conducted by George Hillocks (1987) indicates that such an error-hunt does not make student writing better. In Hillocks' 1987 work, and in the 2007 analysis by Graham and Perin, teaching students how to effectively combine sentences has a moderate effect on improving the writing. This is the *only instructional strategy* connected to the explicit teaching of grammatical conventions or the correction of errors that has been proven to increase student writing proficiency during the past fifty years. The other "broader" strategies of peer response, inquiry, summarization, and writing-process strategy instruction also have proven, positive effects (Graham and Perin 2007)—but marking student errors, teaching parts of speech, and even diagramming sentences, are not connected to improving the quality of student writing.

Written Reflections

My definition of "good writing" or "effective writing" that I would feel comfortable sharing with my students:

_____

_____

_____

_____

_____

CHAPTER 4

Start Using Writing-to-Learn Strategies Tomorrow!

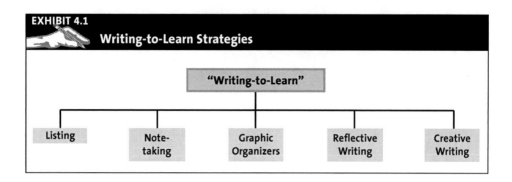

EXHIBIT 4.1

Writing-to-Learn Strategies

"Writing-to-Learn"

Listing | Note-taking | Graphic Organizers | Reflective Writing | Creative Writing

Introduction

Students past kindergarten age generally don't arrive in our classes thrilled about writing. Many of them have the notion that writing is reserved only for the language arts class, and in some ways, their teachers may have even encouraged this attitude over the years by the assignments they have given (or avoided giving).

> ❧
>
> *In order to make the writing process an important component of learning in any class, we must first make sure that our students are comfortable with it.*

In order to make the writing process an important component of learning in any class, we must first make sure that our students are comfortable with it. This takes effort by teachers in building a classroom climate that not only demands writing but has the necessary supports in place. In other words, we must have a writing community established before we can build competent content-area writers. Low-risk, engaging writing must precede higher-risk, intellectually rigorous writing.

The following classroom activities are described in this chapter. All of them are appropriate for use early in the school year or whenever you determine that you are going to focus more on writing. They are all fairly "low-stress" writing-to-learn activities. Academic essays and research reports, two "high-stress" kinds of learning-to-write assignments, are examined more thoroughly in Chapters 6 and 7, and specific strategies aligned with the writing process appear in Chapter 5.

- Listing
- Note-taking
- Using graphic organizers as study aids
- Having reflective tasks to deepen learning
- Using creative writing to deepen learning

Use Listing to Get the Ideas Flowing

Specific kinds of listing activities are excellent to use during prewriting and are also effective to use as stand-alone, writing-to-learn tasks. The best kinds of listing activities to do as stand-alone tasks provide time for students to sort through information they have amassed on any given topic and record ideas to be used later for individual study, cooperative learning, or the drafting of an essay or report.

These three listing activities have proved successful in my own classroom and in classrooms of numerous teachers with whom I've collaborated in the past decade:

- ABC lists
- The "Top 10" list (modeled on David Letterman's sketch of the same name)
- The "Top 3" list with explanations/justifications

A brief summary of each listing strategy appears below. Additional support materials, including student reproducibles and/or handouts, appear in Appendix A (Exhibits A.1 through A.3).

The ABC list

Students list the alphabet from A through Z on paper and then brainstorm, trying to come up with one or more words or phrases from the current learning for each letter. These lists can then become jumping-off points for class discussion or individual or collaborative writing. A variation of this is to simply ask students to number from 1 through 20 or from 1 through 25 and try to generate that many ideas. See Appendix G (Exhibit G.3).

The "Top 10" list

Students number from 1 through 10 on paper. Instead of being as random as an ABC list, this framework provides for a "weeding out" of some ideas, as students have to generate ten items that are particularly important or worth knowing. This strategy forces students to summarize, and, as demonstrated in multiple research studies (Marzano, Pickering, and Pollock 2001), summarizing is a very important skill in overall academic achievement. See Appendix A (Exhibit A.2) for a student example of a "Top 10" list.

The "Top 3" list with explanations or justifications

This framework provides for even higher-level thinking than the "Top 10" list. Students must produce only three items, and they must justify why their list is the "best" representation of current content. Therefore, they have to generate multiple ideas, pare down the list, and evaluate which items are the most important or

EXHIBIT 4.2	
Example of a Student's ABC List from a High School Biology Class	
Animal cells	Nucleus, nucleolus
Bodies (cells are in our bodies)	Organisms have cells, organelles, outer membrane
Cytoplasm	Protoplasm
DNA, division	Q
Eukaryotic	Ribosomes, reticulum
F	Sex cells
Golgi, granules	T
H	U
Inner membrane	Vacuole
J	Wall (cell wall in plant cells)
K	X
L	Y
Membrane (cell membrane), meiosis, mitosis, mitochondria	Z

worthy of knowing. You can then have them verbalize and/or write down their arguments. This activity emphasizes persuasion, which is often a weakness in student writing. See Appendix A (Exhibit A.3) for a student example of a "Top 3" list.

Exhibit 4.2 is an example of a student's ABC list from a high school biology course. The students were reviewing and preparing for a test on the basic structures and functions of the cell. After each student generated his or her own list, the student partnered with a classmate, and both were asked to add to their respective lists.

Teach Note-Taking to Help Students Learn Academic Material

In most classes, students will have to take notes at one time or another. In some classes, like history, frequent note-taking is a necessity. However, many of us who have worked with secondary students know that very often, they do not have good note-taking skills. As a teacher, I have some choices. I can silently lament this fact, I can be angry and share my frustrations with my colleagues in the teachers' lounge, or I can do something about it and teach my students a few ways to take good notes. I have always preferred to take charge and teach them this vital skill—and I do it early in the school year so that they have a tool for success immediately at their disposal.

Three forms of note-taking are summarized below. Additional support materials, including handouts for students, appear in Appendix B (Exhibits B.1 through B.7). Try at least one of these note-taking formats and use it over a period of several weeks to see if it enhances achievement in your class.

> *Many of us who have worked with secondary students know that very often, they do not have good note-taking skills.*

Cornell notes

This note-taking format originated with Walter Pauk, a professor at Cornell University, and appeared in the first edition of his book, *How To Study in College* (8th edition, 2006). The template is a two-column design, with the left side reserved for key ideas (succinct statements) and the right side for details (see Exhibit 4.3). This form also includes a summary box at the bottom of the two columns. Very often, teachers provide some of the material "filled in" on the template and work with students to write the required summaries until students grow accustomed to the form and are increasingly competent in using it.

EXHIBIT 4.3

Example of Cornell Notes from a High School U.S. History Course

Chapter 2
The Beginnings of a Nation: The Revolutionary War

Events of 1775 (leading up)	• 2nd Continental Congress convened • Battles had broken out in MA (Concord and Lexington) • George Washington chosen by Congress to lead Army • One more message sent to King George in England to prevent war; did not work • Battle of Bunker Hill • King George declared the colonies in open rebellion
Thomas Paine, "Common Sense"	• Published • Sold 150,000 copies • Attacked the idea of being governed by a king
Thomas Jefferson, Declaration of Independence	• Two parts: one explaining rights and one listing complaints against British • Main complaints were taxation without representation and presence of British troops

Summary

The decision to declare independence and engage in war was not made lightly or quickly. The Continental Congress tried to avoid war but saw it had to happen. When Paine's work was published, more people wanted independence. Washington was a good military leader, and when Jefferson wrote the Declaration, it was time to move forward.

Combination notes

Combination notes (Marzano, Pickering, and Pollock 2001) are a variation of Cornell notes. The left side is for notes "taken using informal outlining or a variation of it" (page 47), and the right side is for webbing, drawing, and/or words, but the focus is more on using nonlinguistic information. While taking combination notes, students "must stop periodically and make a graphic representation" (page 48). As the authors aptly note (page 48), this form of note-taking may take additional time in class, but students then process the information a second time (nonlinguistically), which results in deeper learning. The form also includes a summary box, which forces students to process information a third time. See Appendix B (Exhibit B.4) for an example of combination notes.

Outlines

There are many types of outlines, but the defining feature of all outlines is that they break information into manageable "chunks": topics, subtopics, and details. Teachers can start outlining with students by providing partially completed templates and then take away the support as students grow more competent. Examples of the standard (Roman numeral) outline, number notes (a variation using only Arabic numerals), and a visual outline (tree chart), appear in the support materials in Appendix B (Exhibits B.5 through B.7).

Exhibit 4.3 is an example of Cornell notes from a high school U.S. history course. The students had practiced considerably by this point in the year, and the teacher only helped them to generate the three main topics in the lefthand column. They were asked to listen to her lecture and skim their textbooks simultaneously to generate the notes in the righthand column, and the last five minutes of class were used for them to independently generate their summaries.

Because almost all secondary teachers require their students to take notes in class at one time or another, these three note-taking methods (Cornell, combination, and outline) should prove useful for the teacher in addition to helping students learn content material.

Teach the Use of Graphic Organizers as Study Aids

Graphic organizers are visual tools that help students organize their ideas—sometimes in preparation for writing and at other times as a note-taking or study device. Having students capture their ideas about what they have learned using a graphic organizer can be an excellent stand-alone writing activity. You can use graphic organizers frequently with very little advance preparation when you intend them to be helpful as study aids for students.

These devices work because they tap into the nonlinguistic areas of the brain while students are also accessing the linguistic areas. This premise has often been called "dual coding." Although neuroscientists would caution us, educators hope that if students are exercising more than one brain area at a time, learning can be increased.

Students should use certain general graphic organizers because of the thinking associated with them. Venn diagrams and double bubble maps (Hyerle 2004) are good for comparing two items. Comparison matrices are good for comparing multiple items on multiple criteria. Tree charts are best for sorting large amounts of information, perhaps at the end of a unit of study. Flow charts and cycle diagrams show sequences, and therefore help students remember the order of events both linguistically and visually.

Hundreds of graphic organizer templates exist for use by teachers. However, focusing only on a few visuals and using them repeatedly for certain kinds of thinking allows students to learn these particular tools well and to apply them in various academic situations. This very thesis has been illustrated in the past decade most clearly in David Hyerle's work with the visual tools called "Thinking Maps" (2004).

See Appendix C (Exhibits C.1 and C.2) for more in-depth explanations of the Venn diagram and double bubble map.

Use Reflective Tasks to Deepen Learning

This type of writing is low-stress for the student and gives the teacher abundant information about how to adapt instruction.

Many writing tasks fall into this category. However, the following reflective writing activities deserve mention here:

- Entrance and exit slips
- "Know, want to learn, learned" (KWL) chart with writing
- Think-write-pair share
- Four-square reflections
- Most important word and symbol
- Processing Your Process (for math)

Each of these six types is summarized below. For additional support materials, see Appendix D.

Entrance/exit slips

Students write these brief responses upon entering or before leaving class, in response to a teacher prompt. These are valuable formative assessment tools for the teacher.

Here is an example of an entrance slip written in an eighth grade algebra class.

You asked us when we look at a graph, how we know it's a function. Well first I would see if it's a straight line. Both negative and positive numbers can make the straight line. I also can tell without looking at the graph by writing the pairs down on paper. That would help me decide whether or not it's a function.

Other student examples of an entrance and exit slip are provided in Appendix D (Exhibit D.1).

KWL with writing

The KWL chart has been around for a long time. For many teachers, it has out-lived its effectiveness. Teacher, author, and professional developer Janet Allen (2004) has recommended a column called "B" for "building background knowl-edge," making the chart a BKWL. Doug Reeves has recommended a KNU chart: know, need to know, understand (Effective Teaching Strategies seminar). Using a KWL chart or one of its adaptations during class discussion can help students gen-erate ideas. You can also model the structure of complete sentences and even ways to cite sources through the creative use of a KWL chart. An example of a KWL chart is provided in Appendix D (Exhibit D.2).

Think-write-pair share

Students are given a prompt or question. The teacher allows some thinking time (about one minute) and then asks the students to write in response to the prompt or question (for two to three minutes). Students are then paired and share ideas from the writing with each other. This is a good activity to use the day before a quiz or test, as it allows students to articulate what they understand about the current content and serves as a review. An example of a think-write-pair share can be found in Appendix D (Exhibit D.3).

One middle school math class used the following prompt for a think-write-pair share activity, then each student individually solved the problem in writing and turned it in after the paired discussion. Each individual written answer turned in had to have an explanation in addition to the correctly solved problem.

Our principal, Mr. Pascual, was standing on the middle rung (or step) of a ladder on his way up to the roof of his house. First he climbed up 3 rungs, and then he went down 5. Finally he climbed up 10 rungs to get to the top of the ladder. How many rungs (steps) are there on the ladder?

Four-square reflections

Students divide a sheet of notebook paper into fourths, drawing lines that form boxes. Then the teacher poses a guiding question for each box. Students fill the boxes with their responses.

An example of a four-square reflection by a sixth grade student is shown in Exhibit 4.4.

EXHIBIT 4.4 Student's Example of a Four-Square Reflection, Sixth Grade	
State We learned about trade between countries and how it helps the economy. Focusing on the U.S., Canada, Mexico, and the Caribbean.	**Reflect** I wonder why it seems the U.S. is well off with money but Mexico on the news and stuff doesn't seem as well off. And I never see Canada on the news. Is gas in Canada higher than here? What about Mexico?
Predict I think we are going to learn more about trade and the things we buy and sell plus also natural resources in each place. Because natural resources like trees are affected when we sell things like paper.	**Visualize** This big dollar sign reminds me that a country has to come out ahead in trading in order to be well off. If you import more than you export you can be unbalanced.

Most important word and symbol

This strategy works best with long texts (perhaps with multiple chapters or long sections of content reading that are hard to read or understand). After reading, students simply take several sheets of blank paper, and, on each sheet, they record a "most important" word (or phrase, if necessary) and a symbol. These items then serve as a linguistic and visual summary of that section or chapter. (Student examples appear in Appendix D, Exhibit D.6.)

"Processing your process"

This strategy, the brainchild of teacher Debra Schneider, has been successful in high school math classrooms in Washington. Students examine a math problem before solving it, write about what they intend to do, then solve the problem. They also reflect on the process and write again. A student handout appears in Appendix D (Exhibit D.7). Teacher notes, along with student examples, also can be found in Appendix D (Exhibit D.8).

Use Creative Writing to Deepen Learning

Creative forms of writing, like poems and essays based on imaginary points of view, can be highly engaging for students. These types of assignments are a good way to begin using writing in your classroom, especially if you feel that students will be intimidated or resistant initially. However, once students are accustomed to writing, they should venture away from creative writing and move to other types. Eventually, they should succeed in crafting proficient essays and reports.

These classroom creative writing activities are briefly described below.

- RAFT
- "I Am" poems
- Bio-poems
- Recasting the text (Fletcher and Portalupi 2001)

RAFT

RAFT is an acronym standing for "role, audience, format, topic" (Santa 1988). After students have amassed a solid amount of knowledge on a topic, RAFT writing can allow them to demonstrate understanding.

The teacher creates a RAFT chart, showing various perspectives from which to write (roles), the intended audience for each piece of writing, the type of writing that is to be done (format), and the narrowed-down topic. Ideally, each student then chooses a row from the chart and writes accordingly.

Exhibits E.1 and E.2 in Appendix E show examples of RAFT charts designed by teachers. Other examples are available online at www.leadandlearn.com/wtl/resources (you must set up a free user account in order to use these resources). Exhibit 4.5 is an example of a RAFT chart used by an elementary teacher in a social studies class.

EXHIBIT 4.5	Example of a RAFT Chart Used by an Elementary Teacher in a Social Studies Class		
Role	**Audience**	**Format**	**Topic**
Inuit	Modern fourth graders	Letter	What life is like for a child in the Inuit tribe
Pawnee	Self	Journal entry	Typical day
Hopi	Seminole	Speech of introduction	Describe self as if meeting for first time
Ponce de Leon	Modern fourth graders	Speech/ presentation	My first experience with Native Americans in America

The following is an example of student writing from a RAFT assignment. The student assumed the role of a point (in mathematics) and wrote a letter to his teacher, trying to convince the teacher that he has a very important mathematical function.

Dear Mrs. Crosby,

Hi there, I'm Payton Point. I am one point of an infinite number of points in space. I'm wondering … do you teach about us in your class? I think you should. For example, every imaginable geometric shape is made up of points. Every triangle, cone, cylinder—you name it! We are very small, so people sometimes ignore the fact that we exist, but we are the building blocks of every shape, just like DNA is the building block of life.

We are parts of a line, too. A line is by definition a set of points. Many people on the street don't even know this! Do your students know it?

Please teach about us in your geometry class. Without us, there is no line, there is no sphere, etc. Your students need to know this!

Best wishes,

Payton

"I Am" Poems

"I Am" poems have great potential. In language arts classes, "I Am" poems are often used by students to write about themselves. Teachers sometimes also adapt the form and the process so that students ask each other questions in pairs, and then each student writes an "I Am" poem about his or her partner.

There are content adaptations for this form, too. After studying any famous person, students can craft "I Am" poems to show what they have learned about the person's life. Teachers have also used this form to have students write about various animals, other life forms, and even geometric shapes and other conceptual topics.

A basic template for the form appears in Appendix F (Exhibit F.1), followed by two examples (Appendix F, Exhibits F.2 and F.3). Here is an excerpt from an "I Am" poem written in a high school geometry class:

> I am a precise polygon.
>
> I wonder if students care about my many sides.
>
> I hear math teachers talking about me all the time.
>
> I see other less complicated shapes and think they are boring.
>
> I want to be known as the most interesting shape with straight lines.
>
> I am a precise polygon.

Bio-Poems

A shorter poem similar to the "I-Am" poem is often called a "bio-poem" and is familiar to many teachers. Students can use a bio-poem to write about themselves or about people (or possibly events) that they have studied. The basic template is as follows:

> Line 1—First name
>
> Line 2—Two adjectives
>
> Line 3—"Sibling of …" (brother or sister) or "Child of …" (parents)
>
> Line 4—"Lover of …" (name two things)
>
> Line 5—"Who fears …" (name two things)
>
> Line 6—"Who would like to see …" (name two things)
>
> Line 7—"Resident of …" (where you live)
>
> Line 8—Last name

Here is an example from a fifth grader.

> Martin Luther
>
> Steadfast, calm
>
> Husband to Coretta
>
> Lover of peace and equal rights
>
> Who wanted to judge people by the content of their character
>
> Resident of Alabama then—and heaven now
>
> King, Jr.

Recasting the Text

"Recasting" means taking something that is currently written in one form and translating it into another form by lifting excerpts of the original and rearranging these excerpts into a new "mold" (Claggett, Reid, and Vinz 1996). Ralph Fletcher and Joann Portalupi (2001) and other educators have written about this form for teachers to use in their classrooms.

For example, in an environmental science class, a teacher may typically require students to write a summary of how a volcano is formed. In this assignment, the student examines a section of the textbook describing how a volcano is formed. Rather than write a summary of the information, the student "recasts" this expository text into a poem using actual words and phrases from the original. In the process, students must reread the text multiple times to select just the right words and phrases and make the meaning clear in the form of a poem.

In another science class, fog is being studied. Following is a simple summary presented to the students at the end of the lesson. Then a student wrote the poem, based on his understanding, and included the terminology from the summary.

> What is fog? In the simplest of terms, fog is a cloud at the earth's surface. Technically, fog is a suspension of small water droplets in the air, reducing horizontal visibility at the earth's surface. Fog is classified into different types, depending on how it forms:
>
> - radiation fog
> - advection fog
> - steam fog
> - upslope fog
> - precipitation fog

"The Fog Rap"

> Water droplets in the air,
>
> Gets all up in your hair!
>
> Can't see up and can't see down,
>
> Be careful when you drive to town!
>
> Radiation, advection too,
>
> Steam upslope—that makes a few.
>
> Don't forget precipitation.
>
> Fog is all across the nation!

Start Emphasizing Writing-to-Learn Tomorrow

Certainly you cannot attempt more than one or two activities outlined in this chapter—and execute them well—this week in your classes. Find several writing-to-learn assignments that seem comfortable for you and that match your current content. Try them out with your students. If possible, ask a colleague to do the same, and compare results. If a particular activity doesn't work well, how could you tweak it to improve the results, or, alternately, what activity might get at the same kinds of thinking and could possibly work better?

Starting on the journey is of the utmost importance. The more you ask your students to write and to solidify their thinking, the more they learn. The point is simply to begin.

Written Reflections

What do I expect to see when I assign my students writing-to-learn activities? How will they react to the tasks? What will they notice about their writing? What will they notice about their thinking and their grasp of the subject matter? How will I address these things?

_____

_____

_____

_____

_____

_____

CHAPTER 5
Plan Ahead to Use Learning-to-Write Strategies

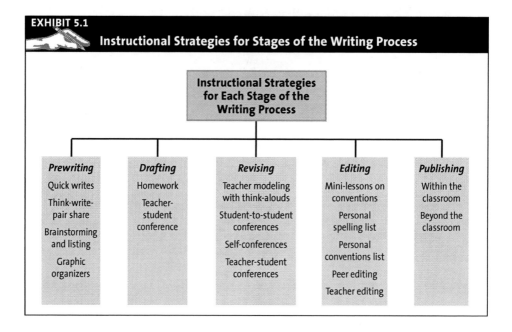

EXHIBIT 5.1

Instructional Strategies for Stages of the Writing Process

Instructional Strategies for Each Stage of the Writing Process

Prewriting	Drafting	Revising	Editing	Publishing
Quick writes	Homework	Teacher modeling with think-alouds	Mini-lessons on conventions	Within the classroom
Think-write-pair share	Teacher-student conference	Student-to-student conferences	Personal spelling list	Beyond the classroom
Brainstorming and listing		Self-conferences	Personal conventions list	
Graphic organizers		Teacher-student conferences	Peer editing	
			Teacher editing	

Introduction

So you have taken the plunge and have decided you want students to craft a published product (most likely some kind of essay or report) in an upcoming unit of study. Congratulations! This chapter will give you advice about how to infuse each stage of the writing process with effective instructional strategies that will be manageable for you and productive for your students as they work their way along to that final product.

The first essential is that you map out enough time for your students to do some prewriting and revising in class. It's also beneficial to have your students draft in class, where you can provide informal, frequent feedback. Obviously, an initial draft may need to be composed as homework because of time constraints. Short editing periods may also need to be interspersed before the final copy is due to you, and you may also want to secure the use of a computer lab (or beg your fellow teachers to assist you by allowing students to use their computers) in the few days before the final copy is due for grading. Unless you are spending significant time in class on all stages of the writing process, you will probably need a minimum of ten class periods (about two weeks) to allow for students to work through all of the stages sufficiently and to ensure that you are also covering required content.

After mapping out your plan, you will want to select certain instructional strategies. Different strategies and activities work well at different stages of the writing process, and you don't have to be an English teacher to use them well. The tree chart in Exhibit 5.1 depicts the strategies that are discussed here; more detailed explanations and support materials, including student handouts, appear in Appendix G and are referenced throughout the chapter.

Prewriting

Quick writes, think-write-pair share, brainstorming, listing, and various kinds of graphic organizers work well in the prewriting stage to assist students as they gather and organize ideas. You have probably already experimented with one or more of these strategies as you have utilized writing-to-learn in your classroom; now it's time to explicitly connect these "beginnings" with a well-crafted, subsequent product.

Your students may have kept some of their graphic organizers, lists, etc. throughout the unit you are now covering; therefore, some of these may be appropriate starting points for writing an essay, report, or other "public" piece of writing. On the other hand, you may be starting a new unit, and the paper will be a culminating assignment. If that's the case, you and your students are "starting from scratch," and therefore you will want to orchestrate at least one deliberate, whole-class prewriting activity. This could be done as part of a class period, with drafting and sharing time to occur during the remainder of the period. Or a prewriting activity may take only ten to thirty minutes, and the drafting may occur on a different day altogether.

A brief discussion of each strategy to use during the prewriting phase follows.

Quick Writes

What the strategy is: A quick write (QW) is nonstop writing on a topic. The writer is not to pause to think or to revise; the writer must write as fast as possible and keep the ideas flowing onto paper.

Why use this strategy? QWs are simple to employ, as they require no advance planning. Students become more highly engaged in lectures, class discussions, and videos when they are asked to do QWs. QWs are a nonthreatening, lively way for students to process information being learned.

How to do it: Start with short bursts of writing (three to four minutes). The first few times, write along with your students; do this standing at the overhead or by circulating and writing on a clipboard or notepad. Be sure to write from a student's point of view (not from your own "expert" point of view). Simply stop your lecture, class discussion, video, etc. and announce a topic or pose a question. Set a timer or use your watch or classroom clock to keep time. Read aloud your own QWs the first few times so that students can hear the kinds of responses you seek.

Possible challenges and adaptations: Because students can take a while to get accustomed to QWs, use them for small amounts of time (but fairly frequently) initially. This kind of fast and furious writing can be difficult to sustain for more than a few minutes; it's important that you be patient with your students' efforts at first.

If you have classes with particularly resistant writers or high numbers of learning-disabled students, start with QWs of only two to three minutes. Let students use index cards or large Post-It notes, as the smaller space in which to write can seem less intimidating for some students. If a student is allowed to use a computer for writing assignments as part of his or her individualized education program (IEP), make sure to allow that same accommodation during QWs. Just make sure that the student spends the entire allotted time typing instead of writing by hand.

If students won't engage immediately, tell them, "I will start keeping time when everyone has his or her pencil moving." As everyone starts, you start, too, to model the process. But be firm and expect everyone to write something, even if only a few sentences.

Advise students to keep their pens, pencils, or cursors moving, even if they have to say, "I don't know what to write. I can't think of anything." I used to tell my students that their hands would never keep up with their brains, but QWs are an attempt to do that.

Exhibits G.1 and G.2 in Appendix G are a student handout and examples of QWs.

Think-Write-Pair Share

What the strategy is: Students are given a prompt or question. The teacher allows some thinking time (about one minute) and then asks the students to write in response to the prompt or question (for two to three minutes). Students are then paired, and they share ideas from their writing with each other.

> *This strategy involves silent reflection during the "think" phase and more active reflection in both the "write" and "pair share" stages.*

Why use this strategy? This may seem counterintuitive, but talking about a topic is a good prewriting strategy. This strategy involves silent reflection during the "think" phase and more active reflection in both the "write" and "pair share" stages. This activity engages both the intrapersonal and interpersonal intelligences of students (Gardner 1993). It also employs cooperative learning, which is a highly effective instructional strategy (Marzano, Pickering, and Pollock 2001).

How to do it: First, students should be grouped in pairs, with the teacher taking a partner if there is an odd number of students. (You can simply say, "You will be partnered with the person behind you" or something similar. The pairing does not have to involve movement.)

The topic should be made clear to the students. Allow about one minute for thinking; tell students not to write during this time, but to just collect their thoughts in preparation for writing. They can stare at the ceiling or put their heads down if you think they will be disruptive or off-task for the one minute period of think time. Then they need two to three minutes of silent writing time in order to prepare for sharing these ideas verbally. Students may write in any form they wish—a list, sentences, a paragraph, whatever. Next, allow time for talking. Students may read their writing aloud or just talk about it with their partner. Allow two minutes and then tell them to switch roles and repeat the talking phase.

Possible challenges and adaptations: If you prefer, allow students to add to their written ideas after talking with their partners. These improved drafts can be stored away as notes or be collected so that you can effectively plan future instruction.

Students who are learning-disabled in writing or who struggle with the mechanics of writing may not be able to write much in two to three minutes. They may need to dictate their thoughts to a person or to a handheld tape recorder. They could also use a computer if one is available during the short writing time.

English language learners can write in their native language, but encourage them to talk with their partners in English. This allows for critical oral language practice.

You can allow students to use diagrams and sketches if you feel that this will facilitate deeper understanding of the information. Encourage students to include writing with their visuals, though.

Brainstorming and Listing

What the strategy is: Brainstorming is freely writing all of the ideas you can think of that are related to a topic or question posed by the teacher. Ideas should not be second-guessed or edited in any way. Brainstorming is often done in list form but can be done in other formats (sentence form, etc.). In listing, students can "edit out" certain ideas; they don't have to list everything. In brainstorming, however, anything goes.

Why use this strategy? Students often struggle with prewriting, and if time is taken to effectively prewrite, the final draft product usually comes out much better. Also, students may have been taught to "filter" their ideas. Brainstorming and listing allow them to explore ideas wildly before settling on one topic. These activities encourage divergent thinking.

After brainstorming or listing, students may need assistance in organizing the ideas. Graphic organizers are terrific organizing tools at this stage. Brainstorming is random; graphic organizers help "rope in" the ideas and create order.

How to do it: Announce a topic or pose a question, and then allow students to write for a specified amount of time.

A framework for brainstorming that was always helpful for me and my students was for them to number from 1 through 20 down a blank page before beginning. I would encourage them to push themselves to get at least twenty ideas about the subject that I would soon announce. After using the 1 through 20 format several times, the number didn't intimidate them any longer, and many students were able to get twenty ideas in a matter of just a few minutes. Some would even proudly go to thirty ideas or more.

Possible challenges and adaptations: Listing and brainstorming can become a cooperative learning activity. After each student independently (and silently) brainstorms or lists for a few minutes, pairs or triads can compare with each other and borrow each other's ideas if they think that the ideas are viable for their own writing.

After brainstorming or listing, students may need assistance in organizing the ideas. Graphic organizers are terrific organizing tools at this stage. Brainstorming is random; graphic organizers help "rope in" the ideas and create order.

Students who have problems with cognitive processing may not be able to brainstorm or list items quickly. Dictating their ideas to another person or to a handheld tape recorder may help. These students may need more time and additional assistance before going to the next activity using the brainstorming or list. The cooperative learning adaptation can help them borrow ideas from others who are faster processors.

For student examples, see Appendix A (Exhibit A.1). A student handout for the ABC List is available in Appendix G (Exhibit G.3).

Graphic Organizers

What the strategy is: Hundreds of graphic organizers (GOs) exist. They are visual tools that help students organize ideas. GOs are either general or task-specific. A general GO can be used with many types of thinking and writing tasks; for example, a Venn diagram can be used whenever a student is asked to compare two things. A task-specific GO is used only with the assigned task, however. An example of a task-specific GO would be a template I would give my students to help them plan a persuasive essay about a particular literary work.

Why use this strategy? Using nonlinguistic tools helps students learn more effectively; graphic organizers are one type of nonlinguistic tool (Marzano, Pickering, and Pollock 2001). When students process information in both linguistic and visual forms, learning is enhanced.

How to do it: Some of the most useful GOs are for comparison, categorization, and sequencing. Select a visual for each of these thinking skills and use that visual consistently. The visual can be reproduced or hand-drawn. The repetition of the selected visuals is important because this repetition helps students access these important learning tools for independent use.

In order to compare two items, use the Venn diagram (Exhibit 5.2) or a double-bubble map (Exhibit 5.3) (Hyerle 2004). For comparison of multiple items, use a comparison matrix (Exhibit 5.4).

For classification or categorization, use a basic tree chart—also sometimes called a network tree (Exhibit 5.5) or tree map (Hyerle 2004).

For sequencing, use a basic flow chart (Exhibit 5.6) or a cycle diagram (Exhibit 5.7). A flow chart denotes a linear process, whereas a cycle diagram denotes a more circular process.

A reproducible Venn diagram is available in Appendix C, along with a student example of a double bubble map.

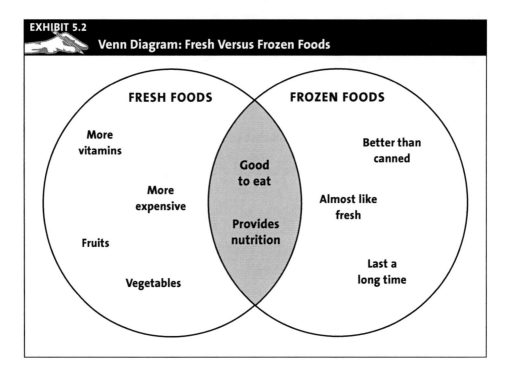

EXHIBIT 5.2

Venn Diagram: Fresh Versus Frozen Foods

FRESH FOODS

FROZEN FOODS

More vitamins

More expensive

Fruits

Vegetables

Good to eat

Provides nutrition

Better than canned

Almost like fresh

Last a long time

EXHIBIT 5.3
Double Bubble Map Comparing Gases and Liquids

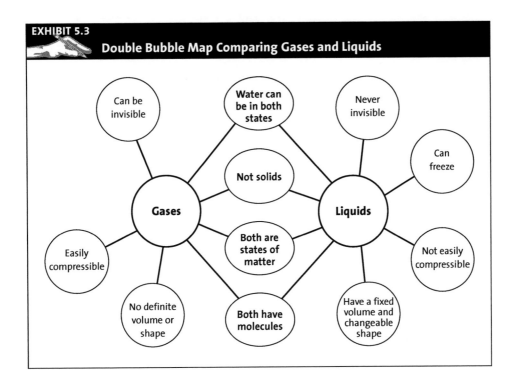

EXHIBIT 5.4
Comparison Matrix: Upper Elementary Music

Composer	Genre	Style	Title	Time Period
John Lennon	Pop/rock	Guitar, drums, vocals	"Hard Day's Night"	1960s
J. S. Bach	Baroque	Chamber orchestra	Brandenburg Concerti	Early 1700s
Ludwig van Beethoven	Classical/ Romantic	Symphony orchestra	Sixth Symphony *(Pastoral)*	Late 1700s to early 1800s

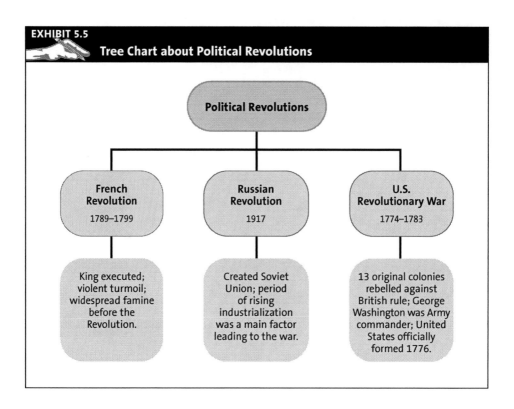

EXHIBIT 5.5

Tree Chart about Political Revolutions

Political Revolutions

French Revolution
1789–1799

Russian Revolution
1917

U.S. Revolutionary War
1774–1783

King executed; violent turmoil; widespread famine before the Revolution.

Created Soviet Union; period of rising industrialization was a main factor leading to the war.

13 original colonies rebelled against British rule; George Washington was Army commander; United States officially formed 1776.

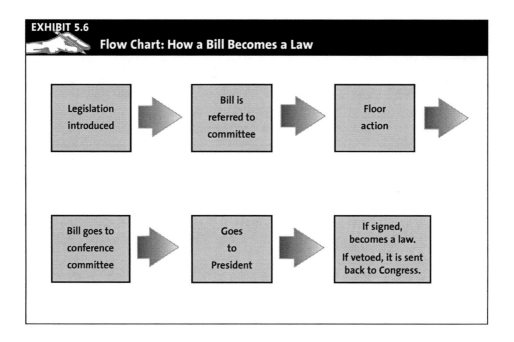

EXHIBIT 5.6

Flow Chart: How a Bill Becomes a Law

Legislation introduced

Bill is referred to committee

Floor action

Bill goes to conference committee

Goes to President

If signed, becomes a law.

If vetoed, it is sent back to Congress.

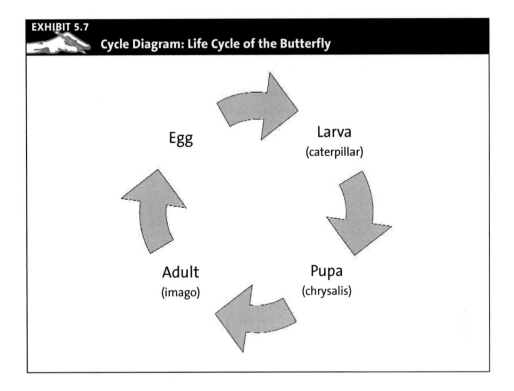

EXHIBIT 5.7

Cycle Diagram: Life Cycle of the Butterfly

Egg

Larva
(caterpillar)

Adult
(imago)

Pupa
(chrysalis)

Possible challenges and adaptations: Encourage students to spend most of their time thinking and writing, not drawing or coloring the organizer.

Kidspiration and Inspiration are software programs that create graphic organizers. These programs allow students to "plug in" their ideas, and then the visual is created. These visuals can also be turned into outlines and other text forms. Go to kidspiration.com or inspiration.com to see a demonstration. Caution: Students sometimes spend too much time tinkering with colors, shapes, and other formatting when using these programs. Remember that a GO is supposed to help a writer organize information, not make it "beautiful." Students must be monitored closely when using these programs.

Drafting

As mentioned before, it is best to have some drafting time in class, where a student writer's peers and the teacher can offer informal feedback—and sometimes, just a listening ear! Allowing students to draft in class can also deter Internet cut-and-paste and other undesirable behaviors. However, sometimes you will have to ask your students to complete a first draft (or an intermediate draft) at home or out-side the confines of class time. There are ways to set up this kind of homework assignment for success.

Teacher-student conferences are also effective during the drafting stage. These may be conducted individually or in small groups.

Homework

What the strategy is: As it pertains to the drafting stage of writing, homework consists of students working on a composition outside of class after the organizational plan for the writing has been approved by the teacher.

Why use this strategy? Homework is a well-researched, effective strategy when employed correctly (Marzano, Pickering, and Pollock 2001). In other words, the purpose of the homework must be clear, the student must be capable of completing the homework without assistance, and there must be time and opportunity for the student to complete the homework. If a student has an acceptable plan for writing, an initial draft (or later, a revised draft) can be completed at home to save valuable class time.

> ☙⸱❧
>
> *Keep in mind that it is easier for students to procrastinate, to misunderstand concepts, and to plagiarize when they write outside of class than when you can supervise.*

How to do it: Allow students to continue working on any written product outside of class after they have made their topic clear to you. You may also want them to submit a prewriting plan to you before you assign any writing as homework.

Possible challenges and adaptations: Many of us probably completed much of our prewriting and drafting at home when we were students (at least those of us who are older than thirty-five)—and with various levels of success. Keep in mind that it is easier for students to procrastinate, to misunderstand concepts, and to plagiarize when they write outside of class than when you can supervise. Teachers have gotten increasingly clever about incorporating both prewriting and drafting into class for these very reasons. Completing a draft for homework, though, is still a useful activity, especially if the prewriting was done and responded to (even informally) in class.

Drafting for homework carries with it some risks and problems for which you will need to be prepared. For example, some students will not do the homework, and some might plagiarize or copy from another student. However, it is often necessary so that in-class time can be spent more in the revising and editing phases.

Use cooperative learning activities after assigning writing as homework so that students get immediate peer feedback on their drafts. This also allows those who did not complete the homework time to do it in class if necessary (instead of meeting in a group).

See the student handout called "Tell Me Your Plan" in Appendix G (Exhibit G.4). You can use this with students before they write outside of class so that you know what each person will be writing.

Teacher-Student Conferences

What the strategy is: These conferences take place in class between the teacher and one student, or between the teacher and a small group of students, as early drafts of an assignment are being written (see Exhibits 5.8 and 5.9).

EXHIBIT 5.8

Example of an Individual Conference

Teacher— Are you able to take a break from drafting and talk with me about your work?

Student— Sure.

Teacher— Tell me how it's going so far. Remind me of your thesis.

Student— I'm writing about the lasting effects of the Civil Rights movement. About how the progress made didn't just help blacks but also helped other minorities and women, too.

Teacher— That's right. I remember I gave you the go-ahead on your thesis and your plan a couple of days ago. Is it coming along smoothly?

Student— I need some more information for the paragraph on other minorities. I have a body paragraph about the rights that blacks gained, and I have lots of information about how the movement helped women, especially in the workplace. But my information on the other minorities seems like it's not enough.

Teacher— Why don't you go talk with the media specialist about that? Just explain it like you did here for me. I'll write you a pass.

Student— Okay.

(End of individual conference.)

EXHIBIT 5.9

Example of a Small-Group Conference

Teacher— Thanks for coming over here to meet with me. I know you're all working very hard on your essays. Let's talk about where each one of you stands. Who would like to start?

Student 1— I will. I've got my plan for writing and I've written my introduction. That's about it so far. I know what I'm putting in the body but I've just gotta write that part.

Teacher— Great! Sounds like you're making progress and know just where you're heading. Next?

Student 2— I'm a little farther than that. I'm in the body part. I have four body paragraphs and I'm working on the second one now.

Teacher— Thanks! Maybe we can all get back together when each of you has the full essay. What about you?

Student 3— I have an introduction and a plan for the body, but I went ahead and wrote my conclusion paragraph. I hope that's okay. Then I'm gonna go back and do all the body parts.

Teacher— That's a terrific idea, writing the beginning and then the end, if that works for you. So now you just have to do the middle, right? It's like you're making a sandwich, and you have the two pieces of bread to hold it together, and now you've got to create the fillings.

Student 3— Yeah, you're right! It's kinda like a sandwich right now.

Student 1— I think I might go ahead and try to write my conclusion and then go back to do the body of the essay. I was feeling kinda bored or stuck after I wrote the intro and now I'm not so excited about the middle. So doing it that way might free up my mind a little.

Teacher— Good strategy. Try it and see what you think.

Student 2— I think I'll just keep going and then do the conclusion last. But next time I might try something different, especially if I get bored or I feel stuck.

Teacher— All right, everyone. I think you're all in good places. The three of you may even want to get together later in class today, once you all have drafts of a conclusion, just to bounce ideas off each other. Another thing I'd ask you to check for is how you're moving from idea to idea between body paragraphs. Remember how we looked at those transition ideas? Be sure you think about how to use them.

(End of group conference.)

Why use this strategy? Providing students timely, specific, and corrective feedback is a highly effective instructional method (Marzano, Pickering, and Pollock 2001). Teachers don't usually have time to write corrective comments on all early drafts written by students. Therefore, verbal conferences work well to allow for substantive, quick feedback (which then enhances student learning).

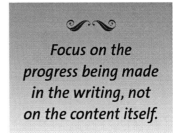

Focus on the progress being made in the writing, not on the content itself.

How to do it: Either circulate through a class to hold one-on-one conferences, or call students to an area of the room for small-group conferences. You can also combine both of these methods over a period of two or three days.

Possible challenges and adaptations: Students can be strategically grouped based on similarities in their writing topics or by common strengths or weaknesses that you noted in the drafts. One successful way I did this was to form groups of three and meet with them as "table groups" in a corner of the room while other students were continuing to work on their drafts.

When you allow drafting time in class, you can circulate and ask questions during the process. Some general questions like, "How can I help you with your writing?" are sometimes best. In these conversations, focus on the progress being made in the writing, not on the content itself. Any content-area clarifications need to be addressed either individually or in whole-class lessons separately.

Revising

Revision, for many experienced writers, is the most fruitful part of the process. As a teacher, you don't want to shortchange the students by not allowing time for toying with their writing, making it more effective, trying out new ideas, and so on. There are a few ways to encourage revision fairly painlessly in your class: teacher modeling with think-alouds, student-to-student (peer) conferences, self-conferences, and, again, as in the drafting stage, teacher-student conferences. Each strategy is briefly described in this section.

Teacher Modeling With Think-Alouds

What the strategy is: This involves the teacher completing part or all of a writing task and showing the students how he or she does it, including speaking aloud to share ideas about the process while he or she is demonstrating.

❧⨾❧

Students may not have had much practice in creating the kind of written product that you have assigned; therefore, showing them how a more experienced writer (and a content expert) would tackle the task helps them think about how to tackle it.

Why use this strategy? Modeling writing in this way is a form of guided practice. Students may not have had much practice in creating the kind of written product that you have assigned; therefore, showing them how a more experienced writer (and a content expert) would tackle the task helps *them* think about how to tackle it.

When students have not had extensive experience in revision or have equated it with editing, we, as teachers, need to show them how we think through our own writing so that we can improve the content.

How to do it: The best way is to actually compose at the overhead so that students can watch you in action. They need to see the ideas going from your head onto paper (or in this case, plastic). Other methods for demonstrating include using the board, chart paper, a SMART board, or photocopies of your handwritten drafts.

Possible challenges and adaptations: Keep the modeling short; students can actively pay attention to this for only about ten minutes. Do not "fake" mistakes so that students will find them (but, obviously, if you do make some kind of error in content or form, and the students find it, that's a wonderful opportunity to show them how one should react!). If you do a think-aloud in one class period and want to use the same writing again, let the students see you thinking through your revisions. You can also pair students and have them do a think-aloud with each other, with each student using a draft prepared ahead of time. Talking through ideas aloud will help each writer settle on the best way to make changes. In a paired situation, keep the think-alouds brief (five to ten minutes per partner, depending on the length of the draft).

For examples and support materials, see Appendix G (Exhibit G.5).

Student-to-Student Conferences (or Peer Conferences)

What the strategy is: Students work together in pairs or groups and offer suggestions to each other about possible revisions (see Exhibit 5.10 for an example).

Why use this strategy? Cooperative learning is a highly effective strategy when it is orchestrated well, and this particular strategy also provides immediate feedback. When writing is being revised, it's helpful for the writer to receive an

---

EXHIBIT 5.10

Example of a Student-to-Student (Peer) Conference

(On each student desk when students entered the room were several peer response sheets (depicted in Appendix G, Exhibit G.6). Below is a description of what the teacher says and what happens.)

Teacher: Today we are going to work in small groups to revise our papers. You'll see on the board that I've written the names of who is in each group. Please gather your draft, something to write with, your response sheets, and anything else you might need now. Put everything else on the floor at the edges of the room. *(Students gather materials)*. Now, please move your desks and gather with your group. *(Students move desks.)*

We're going to use the response sheets we've used before, but I'm going to model this process with you to remind you of how it goes. On the overhead, you'll see the draft I started writing with you the other day. I realize this is just part of my draft, and you have a complete one, but for the sake of time, I would like to use this one.

Please look at a peer response sheet as I read this draft aloud. I'll start by saying that, as the writer of this piece, I would like help with creating a catchy lead. As I read, if you have some ideas about that, please jot them down so you can offer them to me in a minute. *(Teacher reads draft aloud.)*

Jonathan, can you tell me something you liked or something that stood out to you as I read? *(Student answers; teacher responds.)* Tara, how about you? A strength you could tell me about? *(Student answers; teacher responds.)*

Now, Laura, can you offer me a sincere question you have as a reader or listener? *(Student answers; teacher responds.)* Thank you. *(The teacher asks another student or two or calls on volunteers.)*

Now, I asked for help with my lead. I hope some of you have suggestions about that. Of course I'll take other suggestions too. Cedric, do you have a suggestion for me? *(Student answers; teacher responds.)* Tameka, how about you? *(Student answers; teacher responds.)*

Okay. I think you all have shown me you can conduct these conferences. The first reader in your group will be the person whose birthday falls first in the calendar year, so if you have someone who's a January baby, you'll hear that draft first. Please find your first reader; everyone else, get ready to listen. I'm planning for this to last about twenty minutes. If your group finishes before that time, stay seated with your group, but continue revising your paper until I signal for all of us to move our desks back to their original positions.

(Students begin. Teacher starts to circulate.)

> ✑᷉❧
>
> *Professional writers receive advice from reviewers long before an editor ever provides feedback, a fact proving that this kind of strategy is very "real-world" in many respects.*

honest, timely response. This response does not have to come solely from the teacher; peer response can be very helpful and is highly authentic. Professional writers receive advice from reviewers long before an editor ever provides feedback, a fact proving that this kind of strategy is very "real-world" in many respects.

How to do it: This strategy requires careful advance planning in order to be successful. You will need to assign students to pairs or groups prior to their coming to class, and you must be familiar with all students' drafts in order to assign groups wisely. If you are teaching an advanced class or a class with highly motivated, academically successful students, you may be able to let them choose their groups, but otherwise, I don't recommend giving them a choice.

Possible challenges and adaptations: Peer revision is an activity that many teachers try and abandon because it doesn't seem to work well at first. I was one of those teachers for many years until I found a framework that worked for me. If you are a content-area teacher, you will want to save time and begin any peer revision with a clear structure and well-articulated expectations. You might also prefer to work with the English teacher(s) who teach your students and see if it's possible for any peer conferences about your assignment to take place in the English language arts classroom. Many English language arts teachers have built-in "writing workshop" times during which students can work with each other and with the teacher on any paper they are writing.

For an example of a peer response conference sheet that can be given to students, see Appendix G, Exhibit G.6.

Self-Conferences

What the strategy is: Each student works alone and asks him or herself certain questions or uses a checklist in order to revise successfully.

Why use this strategy? This strategy benefits highly intrapersonal learners or those for whom social interaction is not as helpful. It allows for the teacher to meet with individuals or groups while other students are working independently. It also increases meta-cognition.

How to do it: Prepare a list of questions or a checklist, and provide it to students after they have a viable draft of the product that you have assigned. You may want to have laminated copies of this document on hand so that you can simply hand them out when students are ready.

Possible challenges and adaptations: Some students will simply check everything off of the list you provided, or they might glance over the questions and say, "Yeah, I did all that already." It may be beneficial to have these students work with partners and talk with each other about each step.

Modeling the use of the checklist or questions with your own sample draft (even if it's not complete) may help students use the tool better.

Encourage students to use a different color of ink, pencil, or marker each time they return to a draft. This makes it clear both to them and to you exactly how they are revising.

For a variation, you can ask each student to cut his paper apart, paragraph by paragraph. (This works best with a word-processed draft, double-spaced, and even in a large font.) Then you can pair students up and have each try to put his or her partner's paper back in its original order. This activity allows each writer to see if there is appropriate cohesion, transition, and sense of opening and closure.

Appendix G (Exhibit G.7) has a sample checklist for self-conferences.

Teacher-Student Conferences

What the strategy is: These conferences take place in class between the teacher and one student, or between the teacher and a small group of students, after students have viable drafts.

Why use this strategy? Remember that providing students with timely, specific, and corrective feedback is a highly effective instructional method (Marzano, Pickering, and Pollock 2001). The verbal revision conference allows students to get effective feedback before editing and publishing.

How to do it: Either circulate through a class to hold one-on-one conferences, or call students to an area of the room for small-group conferences. You can use the same questions from the peer-response sheet (strength, question, suggestion) (Appendix G, Exhibit G.6) as a framework for your comments. Remember not to give more than a couple of suggestions, because it's hard for a student to make quality revisions in too many areas at one time. You can also ask students to use these questions from the handout, "Preparing for a Conference with the Teacher" (Appendix G, Exhibit G.8), and to come to you with them answered in writing: What parts do you think are not working well? Why are they not working well?

Then you can focus your energies on where the student has decided that he or she needs assistance.

Possible challenges and adaptations: Remember that editing comes later. In a revision conference, you would offer the student writer suggestions about content, organization, and style. If you have limited time, allow twenty to thirty minutes during one class period for student-to-student revision conferences, and on a subsequent day or for homework, allow for self-conferences. If both of these methods are used, you could save time by not holding teacher-student revision conferences, but you would have provided two opportunities for students to revisit their drafts. You could also do teacher-student conferences after these two activities have taken place. In that kind of arrangement, the students would have received ample feedback and should have substantially stronger drafts than when they started.

Editing

Editing is the stage of the writing process during which the writing becomes grammatically correct. It is important during editing that the piece become as accurate in spelling, capitalization, punctuation, usage, grammar, and syntax as possible. This does not mean, though, that the piece will be perfect. Certain conventions, such as the correct use of the semicolon, for example, are not appropriate for particular grade levels. (The correct use of the semicolon usually appears in state standards sometime after sixth grade.)

> ∽◦∾
>
> *A few activities, done well, can get you valuable leverage in the correct use of conventions in your classes. Those activities are mini-lessons, personal spelling lists, personal conventions lists, peer editing, and teacher editing.*

A few activities, done well, can get you valuable leverage in the correct use of conventions in your classes. Those activities are mini-lessons, personal spelling lists, personal conventions lists, peer editing, and teacher editing. If you have limited time and can implement only a couple of these strategies, I recommend mini-lessons combined with personal conventions lists. In this way, students are held accountable for the mini-lessons and also become aware of problems in conventions aside from those mini-lessons; this is personalized learning at its best!

Mini-Lessons on Conventions

What the strategy is: A mini-lesson is a focused, whole-class discussion of an issue that the teacher has found in more than half of the students' writing. The lesson should last no more than fifteen minutes.

Why use this strategy? By effectively using mini-lessons based on actual weaknesses in student writing, you target skills that need immediate attention. This strategy saves time, because you are addressing a true need of the majority of your students instead of simply teaching about conventions that they may already know. You are also using these skills in a familiar context to students—their own writing—not exercises from a textbook.

How to do it: After familiarizing yourself with drafts of student writing, select a weakness that you see in more than half of the papers. Plan for a short class discussion about this particular weakness. Make the students take notes during the discussion, and ask them to edit their drafts for these weaknesses in particular.

Possible challenges and adaptations: Not all students will immediately be able to fix the problems that you have identified. However, you should see the targeted weaknesses decrease immediately for many of your students.

One example of mini-lessons being used across the curriculum effectively comes from Tehipite Middle School in Fresno Unified School District in Fresno, California. After the school had done several schoolwide writing prompts, the students were becoming increasingly more fluent and had greater competency in organization. However, the faculty and I discovered a problem on which we wanted to focus: sentence fragments. With my facilitation, the entire staff then reviewed the linguistic definitions of the words "sentence," "fragment," and "run-on." They collaboratively created definitions and a visual that would be used with all students in the weeks prior to the next schoolwide writing prompt. All teachers conducted mini-lessons, when appropriate, in their classes, and the physical education teachers asked students to respond to roll call by creating complete sentences. In the few weeks between writing prompts, the students showed remarkable progress in decreasing the use of improperly formed sentences.

Exhibit 5.11 contains a list of possible topics for mini-lessons.

Personal Spelling List

What the strategy is: Each student keeps his or her own list of words that are frequently misspelled. This list can be referred to in the editing stage for any future writing so that the student begins to self-correct these words.

EXHIBIT 5.11

Topics for Mini-Lessons

1. Various prewriting strategies

2. Writing good introductions in essays

3. Writing good conclusions in essays

4. Avoiding sentence fragments and run-on sentences

5. Using transitions between sentences

6. Combining sentences to increase the effectiveness of writing

7. Using transitions between paragraphs

8. Citing outside sources in essays, research papers, and presentations

9. Commonly misspelled words (from students' papers)

10. Common errors with commas (from students' papers)

11. Effective uses of voice (examples from professional writers and/or student papers)

12. Common organizational patterns for essays and research papers

13. Using strong vocabulary instead of "tired" words (from students' papers)

14. Effective versus ineffective thesis statements

15. Common usage errors (their/there, it's/its)

Why use this strategy? This strategy provides for excellent differentiation; students practice only those words that apply directly to them instead of learning how to spell decontextualized lists of words. Also, the list in any content-area class can be tailored to specific terms from that discipline in addition to common words (like "separate" and "principle") that may occur across disciplines.

How to do it: Use the student handout, "Personal Spelling List," provided in Appendix G (Exhibit G.9), or simply have students create their own template of columns, as depicted in Exhibit 5.12.

Possible challenges and adaptations: It's important for students to write (or type) the words themselves in order to practice the correct spelling repeatedly. With this particular strategy, then, it would not be appropriate to have a student dictate to someone else. However, other adaptations for special needs students could

EXHIBIT 5.12

Template for a Personal Spelling List

Word, spelled correctly	Practice	Practice	Practice	Hint to help me remember the correct spelling

include using crayons or markers so that the colors add visual interest, or writing words in the air with one's finger, or using clay to make models of the words.

Some students may misspell so many words in any given draft that you will have to be selective in what students place on their list. In a case like this, it might be best to focus only on the most important terminology in your discipline or to select the "top three" words that you want the student to learn with each draft.

Personal Conventions List

What the strategy is: The personal conventions list works much like the personal spelling list but is best used in one-to-one teacher-student conferences, in a small

EXHIBIT 5.13

Example of a Personal Conventions List

Convention: What is the rule?	The problem: How it was used incorrectly	How to fix the problem	My own example of using it correctly	Hint to help me remember the rule

group where the teacher is providing specific feedback, or during whole-class mini-lessons (when each student is required to make a note about something with which many others are also having trouble). The level of complexity on this list can be too difficult for a student to work alone.

Why use this strategy? This strategy provides a high level of differentiation; students practice only those conventions that apply directly to them instead of completing decontextualized grammatical exercises.

How to do it: Use a reproducible student handout like the one in Appendix G (Exhibit G.10), or have students make columns as seen in Exhibit 5.13.

Possible challenges and adaptations: In classes with large numbers of special needs students, a special-education inclusion teacher can be a tremendous asset, as the general education teacher will not have enough time to go into depth with each student. For any given draft, it is also advisable for the teacher to prioritize the kinds of errors in conventions that are being targeted. Your state writing rubric and your English language arts colleagues can be of tremendous assistance in this regard. You would not want to spend time focusing on dangling participles or split infinitives, but might choose instead to focus on subject-verb agreement, for example, because errors in that area are usually considered serious in any polished written product.

Students need a lot of guidance when they first engage in true peer editing, especially in a content-area class in which they may have had limited experience with all phases of the writing process.

Peer Editing

What the strategy is: Students work cooperatively to edit each other's papers.

Why use this strategy? Peer editing, when done well, provides each student with much-needed timely, personal feedback. It also saves the teacher time, because the teacher circulates and manages the process instead of editing dozens of papers on his or her own.

How to do it: This strategy requires excellent classroom management and thoughtful preparation beforehand. Partners swap papers or work in small groups to complete editing tasks. It helps if the writer has double-spaced the draft (either on a word processor or by hand) prior to a peer editing session; the extra room allows for comments and symbols to be written there.

Possible challenges and adaptations: Students need a lot of guidance when they first engage in true peer editing, especially in a content-area class in which they may have had limited experience with all phases of the writing process. You may have to model some editing steps on the overhead with one of your drafts (or with a draft that you have acquired from another source) *prior to* allowing students to try these editing strategies cooperatively. Another idea is to videotape some peer editing conferences as they are conducted (after students get pretty good at them) and use those video snippets to demonstrate to future classes how the conferences should run.

A student handout for peer editing is provided in Appendix G (Exhibit G.11). If you use the numbered list on the peer editing handout, you may want to start by using only the first three numbers. As you and your students grow more comfortable, you can add the others.

Teacher Editing

What the strategy is: You, the teacher, serve as the final proofreader and mark each student's paper. You then return all of the papers a day or two before the final draft is due, and students use your marks as guidance in preparing their published copies.

Why use this strategy? If the written products are going to be shared with an outside-the-class audience, strict teacher editing is often desirable. Depending on the time constraints when you are working only within your own class—meaning that no one other than you and the students will read the products—you may not want to do teacher editing before publication. If students have had ample time and feedback from you and their peers prior to writing the final draft, last-minute editing by you may be unnecessary, since your primary concern is assessing the learning of subject matter, not editing skills.

> *It is, however, an authentic learning activity for students to experience strict editing; that's what happens with "real" writers before anything goes to press.*

It is, however, an authentic learning activity for students to experience strict editing; that's what happens with "real" writers before anything goes to press.

How to do it: Students should learn the appropriate proofreading and copyediting symbols long before a draft is submitted for this step. See http://www.ccc.commnet.edu/writing/symbols.htm for a good basic set of symbols that are appropriate even for elementary students. These are the symbols used by real copyeditors; therefore, learning them and using them is a very authentic activity for students. You may want to check with the language arts department to see if these symbols have already been taught to your students and, of course, explain that you will be reinforcing their consistent use.

It would be valuable for you to model some editing on the overhead or with a SMART board and a word-processing program before having students submit papers to you for editing. This can be done in a five- to ten-minute mini-lesson on any day during the weeks that you are having students work on an assignment that will go to a final publication stage.

Possible challenges and adaptations: Often there is not time for this step. If that is the case, build in time for peer editing (perhaps twenty to thirty minutes in class prior to when a final product is due). Also, connect with your English language arts colleagues. Many of these teachers allow students to work on various written products during "writing workshop" time and can provide assistance if they know your expectations for the final product.

Publishing

Publishing is when the writing and the intended audience meet. You must consider the publishing stage when you make the writing assignment. In so doing, consider whether or not you can make the writing more authentic by having it reach an audience outside the classroom. Even if you are restricted to having a piece of writing be published only for you and your students, there are ways to share the writing more freely than just having it graded by the teacher. Ideas for publishing within and beyond the classroom follow.

Allowing for the sharing of written products reinforces content knowledge and also helps build a sense of "we are all in this together."

Publishing Within the Classroom

What the strategy is: In this sense, publishing means sharing one's writing with classmates and teacher. This can be accomplished in several ways and is discussed in more detail in this section.

Why use this strategy? Allowing for the sharing of written products reinforces content knowledge and also helps build a sense of "we are all in this together."

How to do it: Classroom read-alouds and displays are the easiest ways for students to share their work (see Exhibit 5.14). Reading aloud final drafts to an audience of the whole class or to a small group is simple for the teacher to orchestrate, and, with a little practice, students can learn to be expressive readers and attentive listeners. See Exhibits 5.14 and 5.15 for a description of how to model a publishing read-aloud and for a process to use with students.

For classroom displays, simply designate bulletin boards or wall spaces, and put the papers on them.

Possible challenges and adaptations: For classroom displays, most teachers know by now not only to display the "best" papers but a good cross-section of work. If you display papers on a bulletin board or wall, you can have a title like "What We Learned about Photosynthesis" to show that these are not necessarily just the most neatly written papers or the "A" papers. It's also helpful to display beside each paper the rubric by which you graded the paper along with any comments that you wrote. If the bottom level of your rubric is a proficiency level like "not yet progressing toward standard" or "must redo to earn credit," you may not

---

EXHIBIT 5.14

Modeling a Publishing Read-Aloud

A successful strategy that I've used over the years and have shared with countless other secondary teachers is to model a "publishing read-aloud" with my students, usually with the first "final draft" product of the course or school year. I do this in a whole-class lesson and offer a few guiding questions on the board or overheard like the following:

- Does the lead catch your attention?
- Which part(s) stand out to you or which ones do you remember after the reading has been completed?
- Does the ending leave you with a sense of closure and/or an "a-ha" feeling?
- What are the best words and phrases that you remember from the piece?

I read my draft (which they have probably seen change throughout the writing process in mini-lessons) aloud and ask them to listen and think about the questions posted. Then I orchestrate a discussion based on the questions. Later, when they read final drafts to the whole class or to small groups (which I always do first), they know how to listen and what kind of comments to offer their classmates.

It's also important for my "model" presentation that we discuss volume, enunciation, not holding the paper in front of my face, and other appropriate presentation techniques.

EXHIBIT 5.15

Protocol for Class Read-Alouds by Students

1. The student introduces self and summarizes the topic of the paper.

2. The student sits or stands (his or her choice) so that the student can be seen by all audience members.

3. The student reads the entire text, or, if agreed upon prior to the reading with the teacher, an excerpt (if the text is very long).

4. As the student reads, either all audience members or selected ones for each reader complete the following:

   a. Strength—Write down something that stands out to you or that you especially like.

   b. Question—Write down a genuine question that you have as a reader and listener. This is not a question designed to have the writer "fix" something.

   c. Suggestion—Write down one thing the writer could do to make the paper even more effective than it already is.

5. The teacher collects the comments and distributes them to the writer. The class may have some brief discussion of each paper read while the next reader is getting ready.

---

want to display those. Instead, you could consider giving the students one more chance to rewrite so that their redrafts could be displayed later.

For students whose papers may not be included in such a display, you could take photos of the whole class or of various small groups to display with the papers so that all students feel included. Adding captions to the photos like, "We all learned something!" is a great way to help the less proficient writers be a part of the group. You could also take pictures of students individually and ask them to write their own captions—related to the content, of course.

Publishing Beyond the Classroom

What the strategy is: Any time an audience other than the teacher and classmates is included, this is publishing beyond the classroom.

Why use this strategy? Written products that reach beyond the class itself are often more engaging and more authentic.

EXHIBIT 5.16
Ways to Share Writing Beyond the Classroom

One technique for sharing student writing is to send representative papers to the principal with a cover letter created collaboratively (at the overhead maybe) by you and the class. The class could select two or three representative papers. Tell the students that you want the principal (or another administrator) to know what is going on in your class, and that's why you're proudly sharing their work. Don't send only the best papers; send truly representative papers each time you do this, and rotate the kids from whom you send samples. This kind of rotation allows your administrator to get a good feel for the types of work being produced and can also help him or her get to know students better. The troublemaker who often ends up in the office may have produced a really effective essay or report, so why not show another side of this student?

You can also share papers with other teachers on your team or with other teachers who teach the same class. If you are planning writing assignments collaboratively, then you should plan a time to get together to examine the data (the student writing). However, even if you're not planning collaboratively, you can copy a few papers and drop them into a colleague's box with a short note, inviting your colleague to do the same. If collaborative planning or scoring processes are not in place at your school, simple gestures like this can be a step in the right direction.

You can also select powerful quotes from a wide cross-section of papers and display only the quotes (and authors' names) out in the hall. This is an excellent way for many students to share the spotlight and for you to recognize the efforts of kids whose work may not often get noticed.

Some assignments are appropriate to send to online student writing sites or to the local newspaper (especially opinion pieces/persuasive writing). A terrific site to publish at is http://thewritesource.com/publish.htm. This is also an excellent source for model student papers, provided by Great Source Publishing.

How to do it: There are many ways to get student writing circulated outside the four walls of your classroom. First, let students know if the audience could be larger than just you and classmates *up front*.

You can share papers with other teachers of the same subject or grade level or send papers to the administrators to read. You can also engage outside audiences like the readership of a local newspaper, local government bodies, etc.

Some specific ideas for sharing your students' writing appear in Exhibit 5.16.

Written Reflections

1. What parts of the writing process frustrate me as a writer? How can I teach my students better as a result of these frustrations that I have experienced?

_____

_____

_____

_____

_____

_____

_____

_____

_____

_____

2. Which instructional strategies highlighted in this chapter intrigue me the most? How do I envision myself using some of these "most intriguing" strategies in my classroom in the future?

_____

_____

_____

_____

_____

_____

_____

_____

_____

CHAPTER 6

Essays: The Staple of Academic Writing

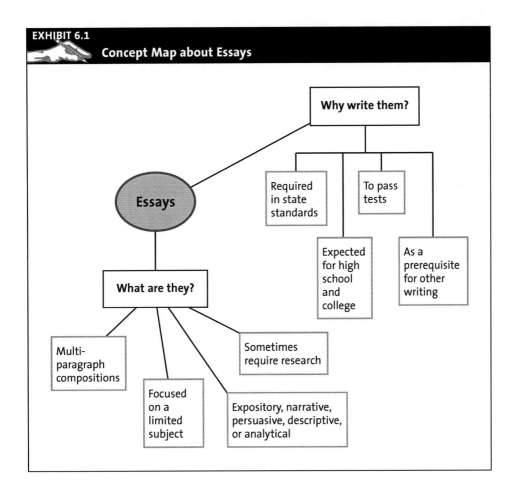

EXHIBIT 6.1

Concept Map about Essays

Why write them?

Essays

Required in state standards

To pass tests

Expected for high school and college

As a prerequisite for other writing

What are they?

Multi-paragraph compositions

Focused on a limited subject

Sometimes require research

Expository, narrative, persuasive, descriptive, or analytical

Why Is Essay Writing Important?

Ah, the essay. It's that most formidable of writing tasks—at least, that's how it seems to us as we graduate from writing single, cohesive paragraphs when we are elementary school youngsters! As we mature, we struggle to keep the essay form lively and fresh, because we grow so accustomed to it and are even bored by it (as our readers often are, too).

> *Evidence suggests that students who engage in writing essays learn more about the content being studied than those who do not.*

It is now expected in the curriculum standards of many states that students be able to write proficiently in the essay form before leaving middle school. In some states, mastery of certain types of essays (particularly the personal narrative) is required before elementary school ends. The essay as a form of writing begins to appear in state standards as early as third grade, and students are expected to be experienced in writing different kinds of essays when they enter middle school. After examining standards documents all across the nation, educator and researcher Douglas Reeves found that by the end of elementary school, students should be able to competently write expository essays and research reports (*Reason to Write* 2002, page 17). Teachers of middle-years students (roughly grades six through eight) should provide plenty of experiences in essay writing for their students, because high school teachers expect students to show flexibility with the form. High school teachers must also help students extend their working knowledge of essays so that the writing of them doesn't become formulaic. Students going to college and those taking advanced courses in high school need practice in writing extended, creative essays that demonstrate ample research support.

Teacher expectations are not the only reason why all educators should be interested in having students write essays. Evidence suggests that students who engage in writing essays learn more about the content being studied than those who do not. Newell (1984) found that students who wrote essays, when compared to their peers who merely took notes or answered study questions but did not write full-length essays, acquired greater content knowledge. Keys (1999) asserts that writing reports in science promotes reflection and the production of new knowledge; report writing is also helpful for students to create meaningful inferences for data. Writing essays is a valuable learning activity for students in all content areas.

Defining the Term "Essay"

So what is an essay, exactly? Even English teachers sometimes have trouble agreeing on a definition, but it's important for educators who are grappling with writing across the curriculum to have a shared understanding of the word. The word "essay" has its origins in the French *essai*, which traces its roots to a Latin word meaning "the act of weighing." An essay is a multiple-paragraph written composition that deals with one subject in a limited fashion, sometimes from a personal point of view (Merriam-Webster online, AOL).

Teachers in a 2006 writing seminar in Savannah, Georgia, came up with this common definition: "An essay is a group of organized paragraphs that support a central concept." A group of teachers trained to lead others in using writing in Sierra Vista, Arizona, said it this way: "An essay is a group of related paragraphs focused on a thesis. Has a minimum of three paragraphs (introduction, body, and conclusion). The introduction contains a thesis. The body contains details that support the thesis. The conclusion relates to, restates, or reflects on the thesis" (2007). Certainly if teachers come to agreement about how they will talk about essays—down to the ways they define the word—this will help students understand.

Let's move from a basic definition to fleshing it out in an educational context. One of the most common forms of essays in secondary school is the standard five-paragraph essay. While this is not the be-all and end-all of essay writing, it is a basic form with which students must initially become familiar and then alter as their writing sophistication grows. It is now good practice to ensure that middle school students are comfortable with the basics of the five-paragraph essay as a prerequisite for high school writing. Ideally, students would enter high school already being able to vary the essay form to meet the academic demands of various classes. With the basic five-paragraph structure in their toolkits upon entering high school, students can meet other writing challenges with success.

With the basic five-paragraph structure in their toolkits upon entering high school, students can meet other writing challenges with success.

All essays have three basic parts: a beginning, middle, and end. In academic essays, these parts are called the introduction (which has a thesis statement, or controlling idea), the body (which contains illustrative details and examples), and the conclusion (which reaffirms or extends the thesis statement and, in persuasive writing, may include a call to action).

An introduction introduces the topic of the essay and, as appropriate, the stance of the writer toward this topic. Inexperienced essay writers often know that the first part of an essay is called the introduction and sometimes commit the error of introducing themselves; for example, "Hello, my name is Tyrell, and today I will be writing about why all restaurants should ban trans-fats." As experienced readers and writers, we might chuckle at this kind of opening, but if we consider it carefully, we can see that hidden in the error is a misunderstanding of the term "introduction." A social introduction does not an essay introduction make!

It's crucial that you check the state and local writing rubrics used to assess your students and learn the terminology. For example, the term "thesis statement"

In California, an essay without an identifiable thesis statement, even if it has five or six paragraphs on one topic, would not be considered proficient.

appears in California's writing rubrics. An essay without an identifiable thesis statement, even if it has five or six paragraphs on one topic, would not be considered proficient. Other states call a thesis statement the central idea, controlling idea, or simply a thesis (without the word "statement" attached). Many teachers wrongly call the thesis statement of an essay a "main idea" or a "theme," terms that are more accurately applied to fiction. All of this terminology can be very confusing for student writers. Therefore, it behooves educators in any one building to determine what terms they will use to discuss this very important type of writing with their students so that students get clear, consistent messages.

Unlike the body of *expository* essays, the body of *persuasive* essays is sometimes called the "argument" or the "evidence" in both rubrics and standards. If you don't teach your students that "body" and "argument" are synonyms in persuasive essays, confusion may ensue.

As far as a conclusion is concerned (although it is not usually called anything else), students must know that it has to relate to the thesis established in the introduction. It cannot be just a catchy way to end. Nor can it be what I call the "Forrest Gump conclusion" that inexperienced writers often use: a variation of, "And that's all I gotta say about that." I used to tell my students that a good conclusion leaves the reader with a sense of closure—a satisfied feeling or even a special "a-ha" about the topic, which was, of course, introduced in paragraph one in a thesis statement. This explanation seemed to help them better understand the function of the conclusion.

The most important step in writing a five-paragraph essay (or any other type of essay) may be prewriting. Once the planning falls into place, the rest is quite manageable. It has even been said that "a properly planned essay will practically write itself" (http://www.education-world.com/a_curr/profdev/profdev109.shtml.) Thus, prewriting cannot be over-emphasized. When students have a variety of prewriting strategies from which to select, they can avoid "essay panic" and can demonstrate learning in various subjects and classes through competence in the basic essay form.

The most important step in writing a five-paragraph essay (or any other type of essay) may be prewriting.

What Types of Essays Should Students Write?

Several types of essays stand out among others as we increase the use of nonfiction writing in our classrooms. These are the types that get students thinking most critically and applying their learning in meaningful ways. These types are the *expository essay*, the *persuasive essay*, and the *analytical essay*. These broad categories have subcategories embedded within them, as you will see in the following discussion.

Expository Essay

An expository essay is informational. It explains something in detail. We ask our students to write exposition in order to ensure that they:

- Know about something we've taught
- Can explain what they know by using specifics, including solid, accurate details and well-chosen examples

One good way to frame the expository essay is to ask students to think of themselves as teachers when writing one. They are to explain a topic so well that another person would understand it better as a result of reading the paper. Most types of reports that we would assign as teachers are considered expository essays. Summaries that we have students complete in class, regardless of their length, are forms of expository writing, even though they are not full-blown essays (and thus, they are good practice for writing essays later). If we have students conduct personal interviews or complete various forms of observations, these, too, can form foundations for expository essays.

Some expository essays require research. As a teacher, if you assign an essay that requires research, you must provide time and assistance in the research process so that all students have an equal opportunity to use the Internet, access print materials, interview research subjects, and so on. (Research writing is discussed in depth in the next chapter.)

Persuasive Essay

Persuasive essays are important, too. The skill of persuasion is one that will serve students well both in and out of school; many of us who no longer attend public school will agree, based on our own life experiences. Persuasive essays consist of logical argument. The student must take a stand and try to convince the audience to agree. If you tell your students to think like a teacher when writing an expository

> *If you tell your students to think like a teacher when writing an expository essay, you may want to tell them to think like a politician or salesperson when writing persuasion.*

essay, you may want to tell them to think like a politician or salesperson when writing persuasion. When the reader is finished with a persuasive essay, ideally he or she would be nodding in agreement or be ready to take action, having been firmly convinced of the value of the thesis. The key to writing good persuasion is to be fully informed about one's topic and to be compelling, debunking any opposing views and making a case for the views presented.

Analytical Essay

The third important type of essay focuses upon analysis. Analysis comes in many forms, and all of them are appropriate for cross-curricular work. The word "analyze" means "to study or determine the nature and relationship of the parts of by analysis," as in analyzing a traffic pattern, for instance (Merriam-Webster online, AOL). Literally, to analyze is to break something down; as teachers, we may remember this definition from our familiarity with *Bloom's Taxonomy of Educational Objectives.*

Now let's apply this idea of "breaking down" to types of essays that we might have students write. One kind of analytical essay is writing about a process or cycle studied in class (cell respiration, osmosis, graphing an inequality, prenatal development, conducting a lab, reading a textbook chapter, studying for a test, preparing for college, creating a Web page, and so on). A process essay generally tells how to do something or describes how something is done or how something occurs. Some good questions to help guide students in writing these essays appear below.

- On whom or what does this process have an impact?
- Are there different ways of doing the process? (If so, explain them.)
- What skills, materials, tools, etc. are needed for this process?
- How long does the process take? Is the outcome always the same? (If not, explain.)
- How many steps are there in the process? Why is each step important?
- Are there difficulties involved in any of the steps? How can the person doing the process deal with these difficulties?

• Are there other processes that are similar? Could you compare these in order to help the reader understand better?

Another kind of analysis is comparison. Comparison essays are widely used in the English language arts classroom (having students compare two literary works, two authors, two literary periods, etc.) but are not utilized as frequently as they could be in other disciplines. Having students think in terms of similarities and differences is an extremely effective instructional strategy (Marzano, Pickering, and Pollock 2001); therefore, all teachers should find ways to incorporate comparison writing, even if the writing doesn't take the form of a polished essay.

Essays of definition and classification are also types of analytical essays. A definition essay must be based on a concept (inflation, peace, democracy, freedom, revolution, symmetry, harmony, artistic or literary beauty or influence, natural selection, bias, etc.). In this type of essay, the writer presents his or her understanding and clarifies for the reader what the concept really means, providing plenty of examples. In a classification essay, the writer takes a large group and breaks it into its subcomponents (numbers, geometric shapes, a genus, the periodic table, a continent, the thirteen original colonies of the United States), or the writer shows how a specific subject fits into a larger scheme (increased hurricanes as a component of global warming, evangelical Christians as part of the Republican Party, exercise as part of a plan for healthy living). Definition and classification essays can be intellectually challenging for our students and, because of that, offer wonderful opportunities for English specialists and other content-area teachers to collaborate so their students create excellent products.

In another kind of analysis, the cause-effect essay, the writer analyzes the reasons behind an action or event or the consequences of such. Generally, a cause-effect essay focuses on either the causes or the effects, *but not both*. The writer selects an effect and then discusses the most pertinent causes of it, or the writer selects various causes, many times of something that has not been analyzed deeply. Some content-area examples of topics for a cause-effect essay are: high school dropout rates, illiteracy, noise pollution, the Great Depression, the Civil Rights Movement, affirmative action, the AIDS epidemic in Africa, the invention of air conditioning or the personal computer, the extinction of a

Definition and classification essays can be intellectually challenging for our students and, because of that, offer wonderful opportunities for English specialists and other content-area teachers to collaborate so their students create excellent products.

species, the formation of hurricanes, childhood obesity, and the popularity of rap and hip-hop music in the past decade.

Another commonly assigned analytical essay is the problem-solution essay. At its best, this essay tackles a real problem related to the subject matter being studied, explains it fully (giving its origins, establishing why the problem is important, etc.), and proposes at least one viable solution. Some examples of content-area topics appropriate for this type of essay are: the overpopulation of an animal or insect in the local community, the near-extinction of any animal, crowding in the halls at school, the high failure rate in certain courses, gang violence, absenteeism, any historical or current events problem, teen suicide, teen pregnancy, and generational poverty.

How Do You Teach These Essays in Your Classes?

At this point, you're probably wondering, "Oh my gosh! How in the world can I get students to write more, period, much less do all of the essays described in this chapter?"

Relax. No one is saying that you need to rush into your classroom tomorrow and introduce yourself to your students not only as their teacher of _____ subject (fill in the blank) but also as a "writing wizard," ready to show them all the joys of composing.

> ❧
>
> *One way to start small is to have students experiment with poetic forms.... Other good starting points are think-write-pair share or other cooperative writing/talking activities.*

What you *do* need to do is to consider some ways to get students comfortable with writing about the subject matter being studied (or, perhaps first, simply to get them to play around with writing, then ease them into content, as discussed in Chapter 4). *You* know your students best, and you know your own teaching style and comfort levels best. If they already write in learning logs or have been taking Cornell notes, for example, then pushing them a little further is a logical next step. However, if you have shied away from having them write—perhaps you were worried about how long it would take to grade the writing, or perhaps you don't like writing much yourself and have been much more comfortable with multiple-choice and short-answer questions and class discussion to assess students' learning—then you will need to start smaller and in more "playful" ways.

One way to start small is to have students experiment with poetic forms (and these can be related to your content, even initially). Other good starting points are think-write-pair share or other cooperative writing/talking activities. From there, you can move toward a certain kind of essay, maybe a month or two down the road—and one that is appropriate for your content. If you know you will be teaching about the rock cycle or how a bill becomes a law, then assigning a process essay toward the end of that unit makes perfect sense. If you are teaching about a period in history that involved some drastic changes, like any period that includes a war, for instance, or some other period like the beginning of the Civil Rights Movement or the end of apartheid, then having students write cause-effect essays is suitable.

When you first mention the word "essay" to your students, even in passing and not along with making an assignment, it's important that you make sure they understand its meaning. It is not a paragraph; this is a common misconception. It has three distinct parts: the introduction (with thesis statement), the body, and the conclusion. Resist saying "beginning, middle, and end"—the more generic terms. You may want to use a visual like the one in Exhibit 6.2 to help your students conceptualize the parts of an essay.

Models of well-written essays, whether done by students or from other sources, should be shared with students so that they deepen their understanding. After your students begin to grasp the form and have seen multiple models, it's time to start talking about them writing an essay. When you skip the "baby steps" outlined, you may be disappointed that your students don't know how to perform up to your

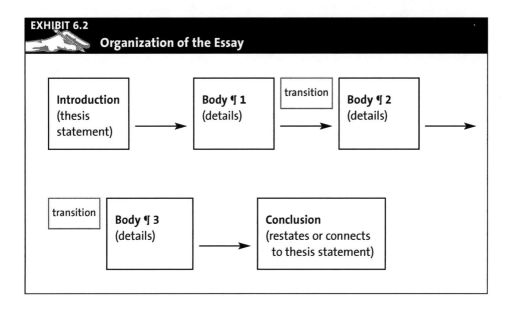

EXHIBIT 6.2

Organization of the Essay

Introduction (thesis statement) → Body ¶ 1 (details) → [transition] Body ¶ 2 (details) →

[transition] Body ¶ 3 (details) → Conclusion (restates or connects to thesis statement)

expectations. Making clear what a good essay is—through models, rubrics, and mini-lessons— is critical before assigning one as a task for students to complete.

In many school systems, students are now entering high school as competent essay writers. If you are in such a situation, you do not have to spend time with the "baby steps." A solid pre-assessment, like a writing-on-demand (timed writing) task in class would help you discern whether or not your students can apply the basics of essay writing to your content area. Simply give a writing prompt connected to current content and see if students can write a rough draft of an essay in about thirty minutes. Any student who hands in a single paragraph, or omits a thesis statement, or does not have multiple details in the body of the essay needs more assistance with this very important form of writing.

Following is a vignette that describes how one teacher orchestrated assigning and teaching about a process essay in her middle school science class.

Vignette: Assigning and Teaching a Process Essay

A middle school science teacher went to a Writing-to-Learn seminar near the end of the school year and decided that she wanted her students to write at least one essay of proficient or higher quality before the year was over. State testing had been completed a couple of weeks earlier, and most of the course content (earth science) had been covered. Upon reflecting on the focus of the course, she realized that her students should, by this point, understand quite a few processes very well. Those processes included the following:

- Formation of planets
- Phases of the moon
- Solar and lunar eclipses
- The causes of waves, currents, and tides
- The causes of and formation phases of a hurricane
- Erosion of coastal areas
- Rock formation

Some of these topics were particularly interesting to her students because they lived in a southeastern, coastal state. She decided that she would allow her students to choose one of the topics and craft a process essay. But first, she had to get them writing to explore their ideas and to see how well they could sequence events in general before she could move them toward writing a process essay.

On day 1, she did a mini-lesson with her students in which she first asked them to silently reflect on their day so far. She allowed about five minutes for them to write on this topic. After they wrote, she modeled for them how to do a flow chart to organize ideas that flow in a sequence. She also discussed with them how important it is to include important details (in this case, eating breakfast, arriving at school, going to class, etc.) and to consider leaving out minor details (such as waving to a friend from the car, dropping a pencil in the hall). After this modeling and discussion, she allowed them about five more minutes to revisit their writing, to move things around, to draw a flow chart, or to revise it in any way they wished. She collected these papers.

On the evening of day 1, the teacher skimmed each student's writing and noted that most of them had a pretty good grasp of ordering events in a process. For each student who did not, she wrote a question in the margin to help the student think about what might be added or deleted. Some of these questions included the following: Did something else happen before you left your house? How did you get from one place to the other? What happened next?

On day 2, the teacher returned the papers and asked the students to keep them until day 3. The science lesson planned for day 2 was delivered as planned.

On day 3, at the beginning of class, the teacher said the following: "You know we're getting to the end of our school year. We've covered many important topics about earth science in this class, and I know you know some of them very well. I'm going to ask you to become an expert in one topic you choose and to write a process essay about that topic. Let me show you what I mean by 'process essay.'" She then handed out a short article from an Internet science site. This article explained how rainbows are formed. They had discussed this topic very briefly in class, but she didn't expect her students to know it very well. The teacher read the article aloud and led a short discussion on how the writing was put together.

Then she wrote the following on the board: "Has an interesting beginning. Includes diagrams. Defines important words, like 'refraction,' in case readers don't know them well. Includes transitions like 'then' and 'at this point' to help the reader move through the article. Ends with a tie back to the beginning."

She proceeded by telling the students that they would be writing an essay like the one they had just read. She displayed on the overhead a list of the seven topics (processes) that she had decided they could choose from and asked them to select one or two that they thought they might each choose on a Post-It note. She collected the Post-It notes. This was the end of the day 3 mini-lesson.

On day 4, the teacher showed them the proficient level of a rubric that she had created based on the essay that they all had read together about rainbows. It said: "Maintains focus on the topic/process. Includes all steps in the process. Has a logical organizational pattern which includes an introduction, body of at least two paragraphs, and conclusion. Uses transition words and phrases between paragraphs and within paragraphs. All pertinent scientific terms are defined and spelled correctly. Grammatical errors may occur, but do not detract from the overall meaning." After discussing this level of expectations, the teacher ensured each student had his or her Post-It note with potential topics and allowed students five minutes to sketch out a prewriting plan. Then she paired up the students and asked them to share their plans, allowing another five minutes. The homework for that night was to write at least an introductory paragraph for the essay (and to go further with a draft if possible). Students put aside their prewriting plans, and the rest of the day 4 science lesson ensued.

On day 5, the teacher opened class by asking several students to share their introductory paragraphs aloud as she circulated to check homework. This took about seven minutes. She then allowed another fifteen minutes for students to draft in class. As they drafted, she circulated and had informal conferences with students who seemed to be struggling. When the timer signaled fifteen minutes had elapsed, she collected everyone's draft to hold until they could work on it again (and so the students wouldn't lose their papers).

On day 6, there was no writing as part of the lesson.

On day 7, she returned the drafts and orchestrated a pair share. She asked each pair to focus on these two questions: Does the writer discuss each stage of the selected process? What can the writer do next with his or her draft? After ten minutes of pair share, students worked individually on their drafts; some used computers in the room because they were finished with a handwritten rough draft. The paper was due for grading on day 10.

On day 8, there was no writing as part of the lesson.

On day 9, the teacher orchestrated a short peer editing session at the beginning of class and placed students in triads. The first reader read only for transitions, and the second reader read only for the definitions and proper spellings of the scientific terms as spelled out in the rubric.

On day 10, the teacher collected the rough drafts that were ready at the beginning of class. For students who were not yet finished, she assigned "homework lunch" in her room or called their elective/related arts teacher to say that she needed them to come during that period (which was her planning period). In this way, each student had a chance to complete the paper on the day it was due without penalty.

While she scored the papers, she created the exemplary (exceeding the standard) and progressing (not meeting the standard) levels of her rubric for this essay. She plans to use the rubric again next year. For students who did not meet the standard, she gave the papers to her language arts colleague and said that the students had one chance to redraft. Any redrafts done before the end of the grading period would be rescored without penalty so that students would be encouraged to improve their writing.

Oregon high school chemistry teacher Susan Weidkamp uses two writing assignments with success. See Appendix H (Exhibits H.1, H.2, and H.3) for more information about these assignments.

You know your students well, and you know your content well. Consider how writing might help your students understand the content more deeply, and think about how you can move them toward that deeper understanding with essay writing.

Written Reflections

1. What content will I teach four to six weeks from now? What two types of essays described in this chapter best fit the content?

_____

_____

_____

_____

_____

_____

_____

2. What "easing into writing" activities am I most interested in trying before using either of the two types of essays listed above? How can I get started with those activities in the coming week?

_____

_____

_____

_____

_____

_____

_____

CHAPTER 7

Research Writing: One Size Doesn't Fit All

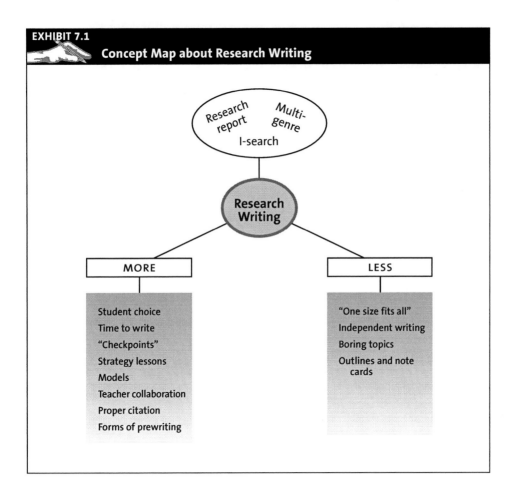

EXHIBIT 7.1

Concept Map about Research Writing

Research report   Multi-genre

I-search

Research Writing

MORE

Student choice
Time to write
"Checkpoints"
Strategy lessons
Models
Teacher collaboration
Proper citation
Forms of prewriting

LESS

"One size fits all"
Independent writing
Boring topics
Outlines and note cards

Introduction

Have you asked your students to write research reports before? Were you pleased with the results? If not, then this chapter is for you. Even if you have found ways to incorporate research writing into your classes successfully, you should find a couple of new ideas worth considering in this chapter.

Briefly, we'll examine three kinds of research writing: the traditional research paper, often assigned in middle and high school; the I-Search paper, first proposed by Ken Macrorie (1988), and multi-genre research writing, popularized by Tom Romano (1995).

General Do's and Don'ts

If you have used research writing in your class before and found it unsuccessful, you may not have fully done one of the following. If you do as many of the following as possible, you will enhance the chances of your students being successful in a research writing endeavor:

- Allow for student choice in the selection of a topic.
- Provide at least some time for all phases of the writing process to occur in class.
- Have checkpoints along the way to ensure that your students are "on track" to complete the final copy of the research paper before the assigned date.
- Teach students explicit prewriting strategies that align well with the kind of research writing that is expected.
- Show models of similar written products well in advance of the drafting stage.
- Teach students how to cite sources properly.
- Collaborate with other teachers (especially special education and English language arts teachers) throughout this process, if possible.

The following actions diminish the likelihood of success for each of your students; in other words, this is a short list of what *not* to do:

- Assign the same topic to every student.
- Assign a research paper without providing time and hands-on support during the process.
- Require the same kind of prewriting evidence from every student (like an outline).
- Require note cards or source cards from everyone.

Examining the Don'ts to Get to More of the Do's

Think back to the first time you wrote a research paper. It was probably in high school. How did this assignment play out for you? Was it something like this scenario?

The teacher announced that there was a research paper due in this particular course, fairly early on. Maybe the assignment was even on a syllabus. As the date drew closer, the teacher announced a date upon which students needed to submit their outlines, and perhaps some assigned topics were bandied about during this time or shortly before. Approximately two days before the outline was due, students frantically tried to settle on a topic, if any choice was allowed. At that point, you may have asked what your friends (who had the same course during a different class period) were choosing so that you could work with someone and perhaps "fool" the teacher by writing pretty much the same paper. On the night before the outline was due, you tried to create an outline. All of those Roman numerals, mixed up with Arabic numerals and regular letters, looked like alphabet soup, but you got an outline created. You then ignored it for about two weeks, until two days before the rough draft of your paper was due.

Sounding familiar? If your teacher didn't require that an outline be submitted before the final draft, did you perhaps find yourself writing the outline *after* you wrote the paper? Is that when you did those required note cards, too—because that's when you finally figured out how to record the information in the proper form on the cards, since you were doing them simultaneously with the bibliography?

Here's the critical question: Were you invested enough in your research to remember the topic now, all of these years later? Contrast the way you remember the senior thesis you had to write for your bachelor's degree (or master's thesis or dissertation) to your memories of the dreaded high school research paper. What are the differences?

Most of us would say that if we wrote an undergraduate thesis, a master's thesis, a dissertation, or a book (and I've written all of these), we were much more "into" the topics of our research for these documents than we were at any time (and with any assignment!) in high school. We would say the process was challenging and joyful (at least at times) and that we came away deeply knowing our subject matter. We might say we had a true sense of accomplishment at the end

It's exactly such an investment of time, energy, and cognition that we need to promote when we ask students to tackle research writing.

of the process, when we shared and/or defended our work. It's exactly such an investment of time, energy, and cognition that we need to promote when we ask students to tackle research writing.

Let's examine the list of "not do's" again:

- Assign the same topic to every student.
- Assign a research paper without providing time and hands-on support during the process.
- Require the same kind of prewriting evidence from every student (like an outline).
- Require note cards or source cards from everyone.

Bullet one seems like common sense, especially if you teach 100 students or more. Surely you don't want to read 100 papers about the same topic; I know I don't, and I'm an English teacher and writer!

Aside from the fact that reading 45 or 75 or 125 papers on one research topic is terribly tedious for the teacher, think about it from the student's point of view. If you remember being assigned a "one-size-fits-all" topic at any time in your secondary school years, you can probably also remember your lack of enthusiasm. Today's kids aren't much different. As teachers, we must teach the required content, but even within the content of any given unit, we can provide at least a few appropriate topics and/or research questions instead of only one. We can also always allow students to generate another topic and submit it to us for prior approval. Very often, our gifted students (or even students with specialized knowledge in any given area) will take us up on that option.

What about time and support? Obviously, your students will still have other class activities going on in the weeks before a final copy of the research report is due. However, you owe it to yourself and to them to break up the writing process into manageable chunks. This will keep them working toward their goal of the finished product and keep you from grading too much at any one time.

If you want papers to be word-processed, be sure to sign up for a computer lab (if your school has one) for at least one full class period a few days before the final copy is due. Once that's taken care of, think about how you will allow students to explore possible content and connect with topics in which they might be interested long before the paper has to come to fruition. A good way to begin is to use the entrance/exit slip strategy and ask inviting questions about what might be the most or least interesting to them in the current unit, or ask them to start with "I wonder" statements related to what's being studied. Once you see where some patterns of interest lie, you can decide how to best direct the rest of the process.

At least ten instructional days before the written product is due, you will want to make sure that every student has an appropriate research question or focus and a written plan (some prewriting attempts) before proceeding. The prewriting plan does not have to be an outline; tree charts and flow charts are excellent alternatives. However, if you don't require students to plan well in advance of writing, and if you don't approve the plans, many students will procrastinate and do poorly at the last minute because of a lack of organization (and a lack of support).

Research can begin as soon as the topic is chosen and some organizational prewriting is done. You will want to reserve the media center one day for research; this should also happen about two weeks before the final product is due.

Now, what about having students keep track of the sources used and about taking accurate notes? Note cards (the way you and I may have learned to do them) may seem antiquated. Instead, have students use Cornell notes and combine information from several sources on one notes page. The summary written after reviewing the notes will help students practice putting information in their own words. You can add a place for students to record the bibliographic information, or they can simply flip their notes pages over and record that on the back side of each Cornell notes page, reserving the front pages only for notes. (A Cornell notes page adapted to be a note-taking template for research appears in Appendix I, Exhibit I.1.)

> *A good way to begin is to use the entrance/exit slip strategy and ask inviting questions about what might be the most or least interesting to them in the current unit, or ask them to start with "I wonder" statements related to what's being studied. Once you see where some patterns of interest lie, you can decide how to best direct the rest of the process.*

Online citation generators are also available for your students to use. If your students can get to computers frequently and easily at school, they can simply enter information from their sources, and software will format their citations on-screen. They can print these entries as they go along, and when it's time to create the works cited list or bibliography for their report, all they have to do is compile the correctly formatted information. Two of the best online citation generators are www.citationmachine.net and www.easybib.com.

Research Writing That Will Excite Your Students

There are two surefire "new" ways for your students to conduct and report research in your classes: the I-Search paper (Macrorie 1988) and multi-genre research (Romano 1995). If you're part of the over-thirty-five crowd, your teachers did not use these methods with you in middle or high school. They both can be highly effective, however, and are worth exploring for adding to your teaching repertoire.

The I-Search Paper

The I-Search paper is intended to engage students in research because they select questions about which they really care. I-Search papers can be undertaken in a content-area class or as an interdisciplinary task in which several teachers engage.

The steps in the I-Search process can be summed up as follows:
- Students become immersed in a topic and generate a guiding question.
- Students develop a search plan to locate information related to their question.
- Students locate and synthesize information.
- Students present their findings.

Students can't do this process alone. In the beginning stages, the teacher is very important. He or she must introduce the overarching concepts or "Big Ideas" (Ainsworth 2003) for the unit and engage the students in rich activities to get them to develop their inquiry skills. For example, students in a high school history class might be studying the American Civil Rights Movement. The teacher could have them read excerpts from their textbook and then juxtapose this assignment with video clips of newscasts of the time period. They could read the poem "The Ballad of Birmingham" and read newspaper accounts of this tragedy in which three young girls were killed. Experiences like this might lead students to ask questions such as the following, which could then be used as guiding questions for research:
- How do people in Birmingham feel about the church bombing today?
- Did the bomber in the 1996 Olympics or Timothy McVeigh have motives that were similar to those of the people who were responsible for the Birmingham bombing?
- Is violence ever justified when people are struggling for rights that they don't have?
- What would my life have been like if I were an elementary school student in the South during the American Civil Rights Movement?

You can see from these few examples all of the different directions an I-Search process can take.

In phase two, after students have selected their questions and had them approved by you, they undertake their research. In this phase, it's important that they "read, watch, ask, and do" (Macrorie 1988). This means that they *read* materials (both print and electronic), *watch* pertinent video clips, *ask* people about their topic (in person, in writing, by phone, or online), and *do* something active. The "something active" can be engaging in some kind of simulation related to the topic, taking a personalized field trip, going to a museum, conducting a survey, etc.

If you are struggling with the "do" part of the process the first time you try an I-Search, just use the "read, watch, ask" parts. The framework of just these three components will differentiate the research you're asking your students to do from other assignments they've done in the past, and will make research a highly active process.

Make sure that students have a plan for reading, watching, asking, and doing before they start recording a lot of information. In Appendix I, Exhibit I.2, you'll find a handout that students can complete and submit to you so that you can approve their plans.

In phase three, students start collecting information. It's important in this phase that you show them ways to take notes and sort what they are finding. This might include teaching them specific graphic organizers and working with them on summarizing.

In the last phase, students determine how they are going to present their findings. Many teachers will require a written product of some sort, but this does not have to be the traditional research paper. If I were a student who chose the question, "What would my life have been like if I were an elementary school student in the South during the American Civil Rights Movement?" my written product might be a fictional narrative about a typical day in my life, or some fictional journal entries. I would have to incorporate all of the factual information that I learned during my I-Search process, of course, but I could use a creative form of writing to do so.

The teacher must determine the appropriate products. In many cases, teachers require not only a written product (even a traditional-type, short report) but also a visual or oral presentation product, like a three-panel exhibit or PowerPoint presentation. It depends on what you're comfortable with when you tackle the I-Search assignment. If you use it more than once over a period of years, it's likely that you will make improvements to it each time. Don't be afraid to adapt it to your needs, but remember the critical pieces: a personally meaningful question or topic, active research, and a product that demonstrates deep understanding.

Multi-Genre Research

Multi-genre research burst onto the writing scene in 1995 with the publication of Tom Romano's book *Writing with Passion*. It has many similarities to the I-Search process, including the selection of a personally meaningful topic of study and conducting "hands-on" or non-traditional research. It's called multi-genre, though, based on the final products. In this kind of research, students present their findings in multiple ways, or genres. For example, I had students do multi-genre research projects in tenth grade a few years ago. I was working in conjunction with a world history teacher, and the students selected topics relevant to what they had studied in that class up to that point. I had one student choose to do her research on the Holocaust. Her final products were a fictional dialogue between a Nazi soldier and a Jewish citizen being taken to a concentration camp, a poem, and a persuasive essay written for other tenth-graders about the ongoing ramifications of the Holocaust.

For more information about the interdisciplinary, multi-genre research done by my own students, see Appendix I (Exhibit I.3).

You could also conduct multi-genre research in your classroom and de-emphasize the traditional research paper. Students could select a topic, have it approved, do research, take notes, then present their findings in ways other than writing. The research and note-taking phases alone provide for critical reading, plus students will experience the important writing tasks of summarizing, sequencing, and hypothesizing. If you have students represent their findings in a PowerPoint presentation, they would still have to write notes from which to speak, plus they would be working in a visual medium.

For support materials on how you could conduct research in your class that culminates in students giving PowerPoint presentations but not writing a traditional research paper, see Appendix I (Exhibit I.4).

If You Must . . . The Traditional Research Paper

You may be required to assign the standard research paper for some reason. If that's the case, here are some tips that should make the process more manageable for you and more meaningful for your students.

1. Strategically plan when you will assign the paper. It's best to link it to a unit of study that lasts several weeks and focuses on critical information in your content area. Also, do not assign a research paper near a school vacation, like in December. If such a paper is due right before a break, you will dread grading the papers the entire time and will end up grading them a day or two before you return. If such a paper is due right after a break, the students will procrastinate, and you will get hurriedly done, low-quality papers. Also, you will not be able to provide students with the support they need in the research and drafting phases unless they are in class with you.

2. Consult your state's writing standards; discuss them with the English language arts teachers if possible. Learn what constitutes an effective research paper aligned with grade-level expectations. Follow the same requirements used by the language arts teacher if possible when assigning a research paper. Even better—try to assign these papers collaboratively, just as my history-teaching colleague and I did. It's entirely possible that the paper you assign in your class can "count" as the research paper that the English teacher thought she had to tackle alone. See if the students can write one paper (doing it well!) and have it count significantly in both classes. Often, English teachers are required to assign research papers and to connect them with the literature being studied. If a literary analysis is not required, but a research paper is, it's entirely possible that the two of you could collaborate, and the students could write only one paper. Then the paper could be scored jointly (with you scoring for critical content, and the English teacher scoring for organization and grade-level conventions).

3. Be as specific as possible when giving the assignment. It's better to err on the side of specificity instead of vagueness. Teacher Susan Weidkamp's example in Appendix H clearly shows students exactly what to do for their paper.

4. Provide models of good research papers. If you can't use samples from your former students, go online and find exemplars. One excellent resource is thewritesource.com. Have whole-class discussions and help the students analyze these papers for what good research writing is long before they have to write about research themselves.

5. Consider making the paper part of a larger classroom performance assessment that includes other tasks like presentations, debates, etc. In this way, students who are not the best writers but who still do complete their research can "shine" when participating in the other tasks.

Written Reflections

What kind of research described in this chapter would I like to try with my students? Do I want to do this collaboratively and, if so, with whom? When could a research project best fit into my curriculum? What topics might be most compelling for my students? What is my tentative plan for using research writing with my students?

_____

_____

_____

_____

_____

_____

_____

_____

_____

_____

_____

_____

_____

_____

_____

_____

Appendices

APPENDIX A: **Brainstorming and Listing**

EXHIBIT A.1

Examples of Brainstorming and Listing

---

20 Things I Remember about Cells
(Biology Class)

1. They are all throughout our bodies
2. They divide
3. Cells have ways to communicate with each other
4. Every cell has a nucleus
5. Every animal cell has a membrane
6. Plant cells have a cell wall instead
7. Mitosis is how they divide
8. Cells have to come from other cells; they don't just come from nowhere
9. My cells have DNA in them
10. Prokaryotic is one kind
11. Eukaryotic is another kind
12. The cytoplasm is all in the animal cell
13. Cells have organelles that do the work
14. Mitochondria do the respiration
15. Ribosomes work with protein
16. The nucleolus is in the nucleus
17. Cells are like building blocks of all humans, plants, and animals
18. Some organisms have only 1 cell
19. Meiosis creates the sex cells
20. All cells need energy

How the Constitution Affects My Life
(U.S. History Class)

- Vote at 18 (amendment)
- Drink alcohol (two amendments)
- "Bear arms"
- Free speech
- Choose my religion
- My land can't be taken by government without them paying me for it
- Can have a trial if charged with crime
- Pay taxes because of the Constitution
- We have a national debt because it's allowed in Constitution

EXHIBIT A.2

Student Example of Top 10 List

10 Most Important Things to Remember about Scientific Inquiry

1. We do experiments for all sorts of reasons.

2. You have to keep an open mind.

3. You have to have other people work on the same thing to get rid of bias.

4. Technology can help with data.

5. You have to calculate correctly and also check your math all the time.

6. Sometimes you have to repeat the experiment many times to check it.

7. Ask questions all along the way.

8. Remember that a hypothesis is not anything until it is proven to be solid.

9. There are different theories to explain things.

10. You have to have believable results and defend them.

EXHIBIT A.3

Student Example of Top 3 List

Top 3 Reasons Students Ought to Learn about the Romans

1. The Romans built some structures that we still build today, like domes and ampitheaters. They figured out how to build things that we still use today.

2. The American legal system is based on Roman law.

3. The Latin language has influenced half or more of the English language. Lots of medical terms and legal terms are from Latin.

APPENDIX B: **Note-Taking**

EXHIBIT B.1

Two Examples of Cornell Notes, Middle School Science

---

1. When is an object in motion?
2. How can you find the speed and velocity of an object?

Motion	(Definitions are helpful)
Describing motion	(Definitions and lists are useful)
Calculating speed	(Formulas and examples)
Velocity	

Summary: Answer the lesson questions using complete sentences.

---

1. What are the 5 functions of the skeletal system?
2. What is a movable joint? Immovable joint?

Functions of the skeletal system	(Give examples)
Bone structure	(Definitions and diagrams are useful)
Bone formation	
Joints	

Summary: Answer the lesson questions using complete sentences.

EXHIBIT B.2

Student Example of Cornell Notes

Skeletal System

1. What are the 5 functions of our skeletal system.
2. What is a movable joint? Immovable joint?

Function of skeletal system	1) Shapes + supports your body ex. spine
	2) protects your internal organs ex. skull, ribs, brain
	3) Muscles are attached to bone to help them move
	4) blood cells form in center of bones called red marrow
	5) calcium is stored in bones along with p hosphorus
Bone Structure	Periosteum - tough tight-fitting membrane. Under periosteum there are two layers compact bone + spongy. compact bone - hard strong layer, makes bone hard + spongy bone - located at ends of long bones such as thigh has small holes to make it light weight cartilage - smooth, slipery, thick layer of tissue, containing blood vessels + minerals, acts as shock absorber
Bone Function	bones form cells of osteoblasts to make tissue. Made of cartilage slowly broken down to turn bone. It also breaks down tissue then rebuilds it.
Joints	Joint - where 2 or more bones meet.
	ligament - tough band of tissue.
	Immovable joints - can't move them, skull
	Movable Joints - moved joints, ball+socket shoulder
	pivot joint neck, hinge joint knee, gliding joint, ball+ bone.
	Joint problems include arthritis, osteoarthritis is when tissue breaks down. Rheumatoid arthritis immune system breaks down it's own tissue

Summary

1. The five functions of the Skeletal System are shape + supports your body, protect your organs, movement, creates blood cells, & stores calcium + phosphorous.

2. A movable joint moves and does something. (example knee, finger, ext.) An immovable joint never moves. (example skull, pelvis)

EXHIBIT B.3

Blank Template for Cornell Notes

Key Points:	Details and Connections:

Summary:

EXHIBIT B.4

Example of Combination Notes

Key Ideas	Notes and Visuals to Help Me Remember
A positive number represents a quantity greater than zero.	Quantity = amount $- - - \, 0 \, + + +$
A negative number represents a quantity less than zero.	$- - - \, 0 \, + + +$
The absolute value is the numerical value of a number regardless of its sign. It's the distance of the number from zero on the number line.	The absolute value of 3 and −3 is 3. It doesn't matter whether it's + or −, it's still 3. (negative side) −3 −2 −1 0 1 2 3 (positive side)

Summary:

All numbers have absolute value that is neither positive nor negative. On the number line, though, numbers are either positive or negative depending on where they are related to zero.

EXHIBIT B.5

Example of Roman Numeral Outline

Middle School Science

I. Surface features of the Earth
    A. Caused by constructive processes
        1. Deltas and sand dunes
        2. Earthquakes
        3. Faults
        4. Volcanoes
    B. Caused by destructive processes
        1. Weathering
        2. Erosion
        3. Impact from animals
        4. Earthquakes
        5. Volcanoes
II. Human intervention/impact of technology on constructive and destructive processes
    A. Flood control
    B. Beach renourishment
    C. Seismological studies

EXHIBIT B.6

Example of Number Notes Using Arabic Numerals

Grade 3 Social Studies

Three Branches of Our United States Government

    1 Executive (means they make sure the laws are carried out and are the heads of our government)

        2 President

        2 Vice President

    1 Legislative (means they make the laws)

        2 House of Representatives

            3 Has 535 members

            3 Each state has a number based on their population

        2 Senate

            3 Has 100 members

            3 Has 2 from each state

    1 Judicial (means they make sure the laws are understood by everyone)

        2 Supreme Court

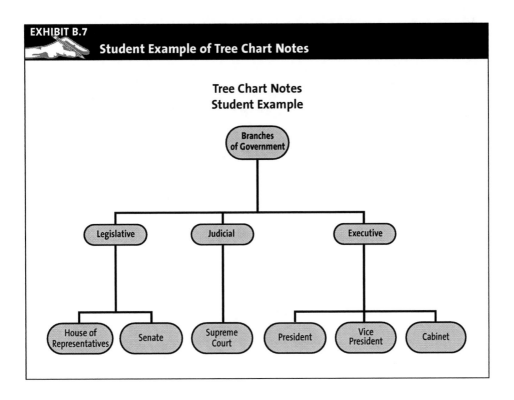

EXHIBIT B.7

Student Example of Tree Chart Notes

APPENDIX C: **Graphic Organizers**

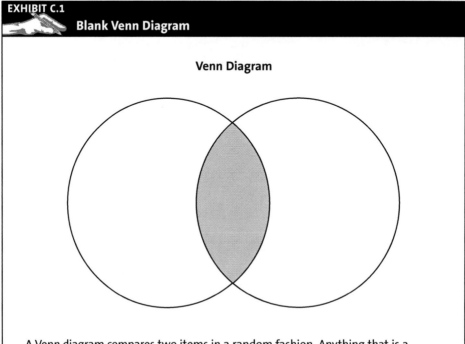

EXHIBIT C.1

Blank Venn Diagram

Venn Diagram

A Venn diagram compares two items in a random fashion. Anything that is a similarity between the items is placed in the overlapping portion. Anything that is unique to one item is placed only in the circle for that item. Words, phrases, sentences, and even symbols can be placed in the Venn.

EXHIBIT C.2
Student Example of a Double Bubble Map

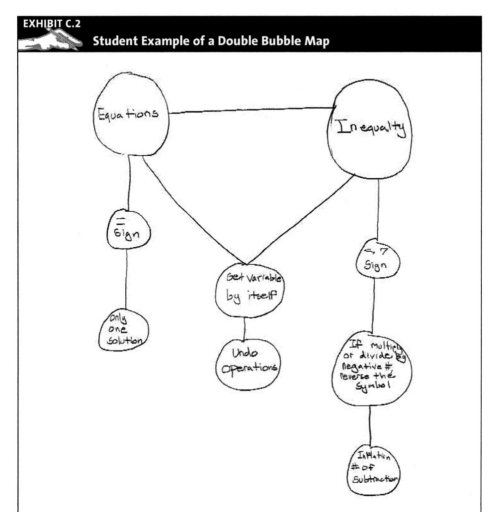

A double bubble map works in the same way a Venn diagram does, but it allows more space. What would have been the overlapping portion in the Venn diagram is now represented by bubbles between the bubbles (circles) representing the two items being compared. Lines connecting each similarity to the two items show the "overlap." Any qualities unique to an item have lines connecting those bubbles only to the bubble for that item itself.

APPENDIX D: **Reflective Tasks to Deepen Learning**

EXHIBIT D.1

 Student Examples of Entrance and Exit Slips

1. **Entrance slip, middle school math:**
   Adding and subtracting positive and negative numbers is not that hard, but now that we are doing the multiplying and dividing I'm getting confused. What I would like to learn in class today are some "hints" and things I can say to myself when I'm doing the work so that I make sure I use the right sign.

2. **Exit slip, high school chemistry:**
   Today we talked about acids and bases. All the time in this class, I learn about how everyday substances are formed chemically—what they are made of, etc. So today I found out that things we have around the house are either acids or bases. Vinegar is an acid. Ammonia is a base. I understand that whether something is acidic or basic is based on pH, but I need to learn more about that tomorrow when we continue.

EXHIBIT D.2

Examples of KWL Charts with Writing

Elementary School Science

What I know about the solar system...	What I wonder or want to know...	What I learned...
The earth is part of the solar system. So is the sun. There are different planets. There are stars and asteroids. When I look in the sky, I see parts of the solar system. The earth rotates.	How many planets are there? How many moons are there? Why does the earth rotate?	

I know a few things about our solar system. Like for one, the earth is part of this system, but it's only one of many planets. Stars and asteroids are also part of the solar system. You can see them in the sky if you watch at night. I want to know how many planets and moons there are. I hope we learn that.

What I know about the solar system...	What I wonder or want to know...	What I learned...
The earth is part of the solar system. So is the sun. There are different planets. There are stars and asteroids. When I look in the sky, I see parts of the solar system. The earth rotates.	How many planets are there? How many moons are there? Why does the earth rotate?	There were 9 but now there are 8 because scientists think Pluto is not a planet anymore. The earth has one moon. Mars has two. Jupiter has 63, Saturn has 56, Uranus has 27 and Neptune has 13. Our teacher had to look all this up on the Internet because it wasn't in our book.

I know more about the solar system now since we have been studying it in class. The earth is a planet and now there are seven more because Pluto was one but it was recently discovered that it's not so it was taken out. There are a lot of moons in the whole solar system but the earth only has one. Jupiter has the most with 63. We are still studying the solar system and now I want to know more about why and how the earth rotates.

EXHIBIT D.3

Example of a Think-Write-Pair Share

Middle School Math

Teacher: "Yesterday we started learning about slope. I'd like for you to think for a moment about how you would describe the concept of slope if we had a new student who just entered our class today. So I'm going to give you about thirty seconds of silent think time." (Time passes.)

"Now, I'd like for you to write for two minutes about what you might say to that student. Just define slope in your own words as best you can, and give examples if you have them." (Time passes.)

"Okay, the two minutes are up. Please finish your last thought. Now we're going to match up in pairs and talk through our ideas. You don't have to read what you wrote to your partner; you can just talk about it. If you want to read it, that's fine too. We're going to talk for about one minute each. So please match up with the person directly behind or beside you. Show me who your partner is by pulling your chairs elbow to elbow." (Students move.) "The person who will talk first is the person with the birthday that occurs earliest in the calendar year. Please raise your hand if you are that person." (Teacher waits.) "Okay, the first person will talk for one minute, and then I'll blink the lights, and then the other person will go. Ready?" (Time passes, students talk, etc.)

Example of what one student wrote:

Slope just means how steep a line is. Like a hill. If it's a steep hill, it's more straight up than flat. So in math slope is based on a formula that we're going to learn more about, and you can graph a line and then figure out its slope. But we haven't done that yet. I do know you can have positive or negative slope depending on which direction the line is going.

EXHIBIT D.4

Student Handout for Four-Square Reflections

Four-Square Reflections

STATE (Tell what you know or what you learned.)	**REFLECT** (Make connections to other learning, use "I wonder" statements, and pose questions.
PREDICT (What do you think we will study next? How will tomorrow's lesson connect to today's?)	**VISUALIZE** (Create a visual that will help you remember what you learned.)

EXHIBIT D.4

Student Handout for Four-Square Reflections *(continued)*

Template for Four-Square Reflections

STATE	REFLECT

PREDICT	VISUALIZE

EXHIBIT D.5

Student Example of Four-Square Reflections

STATE	REFLECT
A fraction represents parts and a whole. The numerator is the top part and is part of the whole which is the bottom or the denominator. So if I had a pizza to share with my friends after school today it could have 8 slices and I would want 2. That would be 2/8. But maybe one friend wanted 4 slices and his fraction would be 4/8 with the top part being not the whole amount but the bottom number is.	When I learned about ratios it was kinda like this because it had two numbers and they were related to each other and together they made a whole number. For example the ratio of teachers and students in this class is one teacher to about 25 students so if you were going to make that a fraction you could say the teacher is 1 person out of 26 people and that could be a fraction of 1/26.
PREDICT	**VISUALIZE**
I think we are going to keep working on our fractions because we are not that good at them yet. Expecially we can't add them very well yet.	 I can remember that this shows 1/4 so I could have one friend over and we could probably have 2 slices each.

EXHIBIT D.6

Student Examples of Most Important Word/Symbol

Example 1

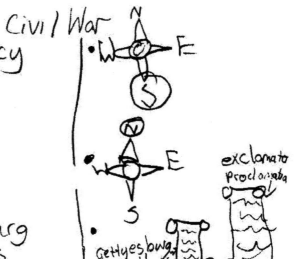

- Confederacy

- Union

- Gettyesburg Adress

Example 2

- Great Migration

- Ellis Island

- Immigration coming to USA

EXHIBIT D.7

Student Handout for Processing Your Process

Name _____

Date _____ Period _____

Processing Your Process

The Task	What do I know about . . .?
Reflection/Analysis	**Reasonableness & Correctness**

	EVIDENCE	Task	What Do I Know?	Reflection/ Analysis	Reasonable & Correctness
For Teacher Use Only	Complete				
	Partial				
	None				

Process Your Process © Debra Schneider 9/2005

EXHIBIT D.8   Teacher Notes and Prompts, Plus Student Example, for Processing Your Process

Processing Your Process Protocol   TEACHER NOTES

∞ ∞

Process Your Process, PYP, is a metacognitive formative assessment. Use this after students have been repeatedly exposed to concepts (through classwork, homework, review problems, etc.). I usually write a prompt that covers about 3 sections of our textbook. Write a problem that has many points of entry.

For example:

> From Algebra 1 Section 5-7
>
> Find the area of the figure formed by joining the points
> A(-4, -3), B(3, -3), C(1, 4), and D(-2, 4)
> Connect them in order. Connect A and D.

In the beginning it helps to give students a structure, the PYP quadrants, to write each part of the PYP. There are four parts.

Some students mix up what goes in the "What Do I Know About" and "Reflection/Analysis" boxes. That's fine.

After I give the first PYP, while training my students, I will show them examples of student work that is both good and not so good. As a class, we discuss what works and what doesn't. This improves the papers.

After that, I do not grade them. I might give points for completion. I sort the collected papers into stacks. There are three outcomes. Most students did not demonstrate understanding, some demonstrate understanding, or most demonstrate understanding.

If students did not demonstrate understanding, then reteaching is necessary.

If some demonstrate understanding , then I match up pairs or groups of students who demonstrated understanding with ones who are not yet understanding. They work together on a review assignment.

I'm still waiting for the day when most demonstrate understanding.

**EXHIBIT D.8   Teacher Notes and Prompts, Plus Student Example,
for Processing Your Process** *(continued)*

TEACHER PROMPTS

Processing Your Process

The Task	What do I know about . . .?
What are you asked to find? Restate the problem in your own words. What information is given?	Draw a diagram, if appropriate. Identify formulas needed to solve. Describe a process you can use to solve. Can you estimate the answer? (An estimate is not a guess). Solve the problem if you can.
Reflection/Analysis	**Reasonableness & Correctness**
Did you do what the problem asked? Explain your process using words and/or pictures or diagrams. What are your questions? Where did you get stuck?	Does your answer seem reasonable? Do you think your answer is correct? Is your answer close to your estimate? Can you get the same answer using another method?

Process Your Process © Debra Schneider 9/2005

EXHIBIT D.8   Teacher Notes and Prompts, Plus Student Example, for Processing Your Process *(continued)*

TEACHER PROMPTS

Processing Your Process

From Algebra 1 Section 5-7

> Find the area of the figure formed by joining the points
> A(-4, -3), B(3, -3), C(1, 4), and D(-2, 4)
> Connect them in order. Connect A and D.

The Task	**What do I know about . . .?**
Sample Find the area of the figure. Graph the points. Join the points to make a figure.	GRAPH The shape is a trapezoid because one pair of sides are parallel. $a = \frac{1}{2} h (b_1 \times b_2).$ By counting the squares I estimate the area is ....
Reflection/Analysis	**Reasonableness & Correctness**
Did you do what the problem asked? Explain your process using words and/or pictures or diagrams. What are your questions? Where did you get stuck?	Does your answer seem reasonable? Do you think your answer is correct? Is your answer close to your estimate? Can you get the same answer using another method?

Process Your Process © Debra Schneider 9/2005

EXHIBIT D.8 **Teacher Notes and Prompts, Plus Student Example, for Processing Your Process** *(continued)*

Name Ben Ryan

Date 9/19/06 **Period** 4

Processing Your Process: Student Example

The Task

How fast should you go to reach school in ⅓ of the time from 30 minutes?

It gives you the original time it takes at the original speed

What do I know about . . .?

This If you have to cut the time in ⅓, it will be 10 minutes. So what you do to one factor, you must do to the other.

$$\frac{30 \text{ min.}}{3} = 10$$

$$\frac{20 \text{ mph}}{3} = 6.\overline{66}$$

But going slower won't get you there faster. So you have to add, 6.66 twice to 20 to get the speed you need to know.

20 + 6.66 + 6.66 = 33.32 mph

Reflection/Analysis

The only thing I got stuck on for a few seconds was:
"Was it a ⅓ of 30 to make 20, or just ⅓ to make 10.

I think I did it right.

This is b/c ⅓ of 30 is 10. So you need to travel at X mph to make the equivalent of 10. So you take ⅓ of 20 and add it 2 times, to get 33.32.

Reasonableness & Correctness

It is unreasonable. I made a mistake.

$$\frac{30}{3} = 10 \text{ min.}$$

$$20 \cdot 3 = 60 \text{ mph.}$$

If you want to get to school 3x faster, you have to go 3x faster, so you must travel 60 MPH! Not 33.32 mph.

For Teacher Use Only	EVIDENCE	Task	What Do I Know?	Reflection/ Analysis	Reasonable & Correctness
	Complete			✓	✓
	Partial	✓	✓		
	None				

Process Your Process © Debra Schneider 9/2005

APPENDIX E: **RAFT Charts**

EXHIBIT E.1

Example of a RAFT Chart Designed by Teachers

Role	Audience	Format	Topic
A plant	The sun	Thank-you note	For the sun's role in the plant's growth
A tree	Students in our school	A speech	How trees and humans work together in photosynthesis
A raindrop	Kindergartners	A letter for their teacher to read aloud to them	Why rain is good for people and the earth

EXHIBIT E.2

Example of a RAFT Chart Designed by Teachers

Role	Audience	Format	Topic
A potato chip	Another potato chip	Dialogue	How the chip will flow through the digestive system
A young child	Parent	Dialogue	"What happens to the food I eat?"
Drug and alcohol counselor	Teenagers	Speech	How alcohol goes through your digestive system and affects your organs, including your brain
A dietitian	Middle school students	Presentation	What you should eat each day and why

EXHIBIT E.3	Example of a RAFT Chart Designed for a Fourth Grade Social Studies Class		
Role	**Audience**	**Format**	**Topic**
Sailor on a whaling ship	The Captain of your ship	Letter	The hardship of having to buy supplies from him
Resident of Nantucket today	Tourists	Poster	Description of reasons to visit Nantucket
Petticoat Row Merchant	Husband away at sea	Journal entry	Life in Nantucket with him gone

EXHIBIT E.4	Example of a RAFT Chart Designed for a Fourth Grade Social Studies Class		
Role	**Audience**	**Format**	**Topic**
Native American	French Explorers	Brochure	How to hunt wisely and not waste anything
Jacques Cartier	Samuel Champlain	Letter	Description of his successful exploration
French Reporter	Louis XIV, King of France	Newspaper Article	Cavaliers discovery of *Louisiane*

APPENDIX F: **"I Am" Poems**

EXHIBIT F.1

Student Handout for Writing an "I Am" Poem

Write an "I Am" Poem

Write a poem following the template.
Follow any other directions the teacher gives you.

FIRST STANZA:

I am _____ and _____ (name two special characteristics)

I wonder _____ (put in something about which you are curious)

I hear _____ (insert a sound)

I see _____ (insert a sight)

I want _____ (insert a desire or goal)

(Repeat the first line of the poem here.)

SECOND STANZA:

I pretend _____ (put in something you pretend to do)

I feel _____ (insert an emotion)

I touch _____ (put in something tangible or intangible)

I worry _____ (put in something that bothers you)

I cry _____ (add something that makes you sad)

(Repeat the first line of the poem here.)

THIRD STANZA:

I understand _____ (put in something you know is true)

I say _____ (write something you believe in)

I dream _____ (write something you dream about or a goal)

I try _____ (write something you make an effort about)

I hope _____ (write something you hope for)

(Repeat the first line of the poem here.)

EXHIBIT F.2

Example of an "I Am" Poem by a Middle School Teacher

Here is an example a middle school teacher wrote to introduce herself to her students at the beginning of the school year.

I am energetic and caring.

I wonder why there is suffering in the world, apathy at my school, and cancer.

I hear the laughter of my students and the shrill sound of the bell to end class.

I see the beautiful blue skies and clear water all around us in our coastal community.

I want to help all my students learn.

I am energetic and caring.

I pretend to like Slim Fast for lunch.

I feel happy most of the time.

I touch the furry ears of my Labrador retrievers when I get home every day.

I worry that my children won't get scholarships to college and I'll never get to retire.

I cry when people mistreat animals.

I am energetic and caring.

I understand that life isn't really fair and there's "no free lunch."

I say that all are created equal.

I dream about world peace.

I try to help others every single day.

I hope my children will experience a better adulthood than I myself have had.

I am energetic and caring.

EXHIBIT F.3

Example of an "I Am" Poem by a High School Geometry Student

I am a precise polygon.
I wonder if students care about my many sides.
I hear math teachers talking about me all the time.
I see other less complicated shapes and think they are boring.
I want to be known as the most interesting shape with straight lines.
I am a precise polygon.

I pretend that I'm a circle sometimes, but no one buys it.
I feel strong and diverse, because I can appear in many places.
I touch points on a line and acute angles.
I worry about people appreciating the beauty of my geometry.
I cry when students get frustrated over me.
I am a precise polygon.

I understand that the world needs me.
I say polygons are very important.
I dream of being appreciated for my beauty and mathematical elegance.
I try to help geometry students all over the world see how lovely I am.
I am a precise polygon!
I am a zany, friendly person!

APPENDIX G: **Learning-to-Write**

EXHIBIT G.1

Student Handout for Quick Writes

Quick Writes

What's a Quick Write (QW)?

A QW is nonstop writing on a topic. The teacher will announce a question or topic, and the student then writes for a short period of time, recording all ideas that come to mind.

Why should we do QWs?

When you record your ideas in writing, you're likely to remember them better.

Are QWs graded?

Sometimes, the teacher will collect your QWs so he or she can see how well you know the material being learned in class. You may or may not get some kind of credit when the teacher collects the papers. Even though the teacher may give you participation or completion credit, QWs are never "graded" for spelling, punctuation, and other errors.

"Rules" for Quick Writes:

1. Keep your hand moving. Even if you have to write, "I don't know what to say next" or something similar, keep writing until you find that next idea related to the content. Make an effort to write for the entire period of the QW, which will be only a few minutes.

2. Don't edit as you go. If you know you misspelled something or used the wrong word, for example, just cross it through with a straight line and keep going. Don't waste time erasing and making your words "perfect."

3. Experiment! Ask questions and play with ideas that you have. This is the time to wonder and reflect on your learning.

Student QW

Topic: Sustained silent reading in an English language arts class

Silent sustained reading. SSR. Why do teachers make us do this? What are the benefits? Hmm, I'm supposed to be arguing for or against having SSR time in class. This is a hard topic. I like SSR myself but know that my friends sometimes hate it. They say they get board reading. It's only 20 mins or something so I don't know why they can't hang in there and just read. Duh. You just have to sit still and do it. Yep like Nike says, just do it! I guess if you read more you get to be a better reader. Thats why our teachers want us to do it. I wonder if thats really true. What if I never did SSR??? Would I forget how to read? No. I don't think so. But getting better at reading is one benefit of SSR. Now I have to think of some others . . .

Student QW

Topic: What you learned/remember from our current science unit

We just learned about mammals. I don't know what all I know about them but I have to write now so I will try to say some stuff about them. They all have hair or fur. People have hair of course but other mammals like cats and dogs and cows and stuff have fur instead of hair. They all feed their babies milk from the mother. They are warm blooded not cold blooded like fish. That means the body temp stays the same and doesn't change based on the environment. There is some big word I can't remember about the warm blood but I guess I'll have to know that for the test. That's all I can remember right now but we still have to write. OK, I'll list some mammals. People, cats, dogs, cows, pigs, whales even though it seems like they are fish they are not.

Student QW

Topic: What do you know about perimeter and area?

Perimeter and area are both measurements but they are different. Perimeter means around the edges. Area is all the space inside, like inside the edges. It's easy to get these confused and on a test, they might try to get you confused, especially if it's multiple choice because it could ask you about area and have the perimeter answer in the choices. For area you have to multiply and for perimeter you just add.

EXHIBIT G.3

Student Handout for the ABC List

ABC List

DIRECTIONS: Your teacher will state a prompt or pose a question. Try to think of related ideas and topics that begin with each letter of the alphabet. You can have more than one idea in each box, and it's okay if you leave a box blank, but try to generate as many ideas as you can.

A	N
B	O
C	P
D	Q
E	R
F	S
G	T
H	U
I	V
J	W
K	X
L	Y
M	Z

EXHIBIT G.4

Student Handout for Tell Me Your Plan

Tell Me Your Plan

Your Name _____

Today's Date _____

Today's homework assignment is that you write a complete first draft. I need some information about what you are writing. Please answer the questions below and turn this sheet in. When I receive your first draft, I will staple this sheet to it and may also need to have a brief conference with you at that time.

1. What is your topic (in a word or phrase)?

2. Do you have some titles in mind for your paper? If so, please share them here. If not, please explain why not.

3. Describe your organizational plan. You may tell me in sentences, by using a graphic organizer, or by using any combination of words and visuals, but make sure I can read and understand this plan!

EXHIBIT G.5

Examples Showing the Use of Think-Alouds

Math Class

Writing prompt: In a paragraph, explain to a classmate how to find the square root of 1600.

First Draft	Think-Aloud
There are different ways to find the square root of 1600, but I will tell you one. I would start with numbers that go into 16. Why 16? Because I took the zeros off to make it easier. I came up with 4. You know 4 x 4 is 16. So then I wonder if 40 x 40 would be 1600. I can write that out or use a calculator and check it, and what do you know, I was right! So my conclusion is that the square root of 1600 is 40.	• I think my first sentence gets the job done but is a little boring. • I could make the middle of the paragraph flow better; seems kind of choppy. • I think I need an ending sentence that's better than the one I have.

Second draft:

   I know at least one way to explain how to find the square root of 1600. Start with numbers that go into 16. Why 16? Because taking the zeros off makes it easier. Then you get 4 because you know 4 x 4 is 16. So I wonder if 40 x 40 would be 1600. I can write that out or use a calculator and check it, and what do you know, I was right! What is YOUR way to find the answer—do you like my ideas, or do you have your own?

Art Class

Writing prompt: What color is most like you? Why?

First Draft	Think-Aloud
I think I'm red—fiery, passionate, high-energy. Red is movement. Red is life. Blood is red, and blood is necessary for human life. It pumps through our bodies and sustains us. Red is also the color of love. Love is one of my favorite topics, too. The love I have in my life is important to me. I am red—decisive and bold at times. I am rarely apathetic. I usually strongly like or dislike things. Even though red is a color, and I'm a living, breathing human being, we have much in common.	• I don't really have an introduction that restates the prompt and lets the reader know what I'm getting ready to write about. • I don't have enough detail about the connection of red and love. • I like the 3rd paragraph and want to expand it. • I like comparing myself to something kind of intangible, like a color, but I probably need to expand the conclusion.

EXHIBIT G.6

Peer Response Conference Sheets for Students

Peer Conference Sheets

Writer's name: _____

As the writer of this piece, I would like help with _____

_____

Listener's name: _____

_____

As the listener for this writer, I share these comments: _____

_____

One thing that I liked or that stood out to me was _____

_____

One question I have is _____

_____

I suggest you _____

_____

The writer decides what to do next. Doing nothing is NOT an option!

Writer's name: _____

As the writer of this piece, I would like help with _____

_____

Listener's name: _____

_____

As the listener for this writer, I share these comments: _____

_____

One thing that I liked or that stood out to me was _____

_____

One question I have is _____

_____

I suggest you _____

_____

The writer decides what to do next. Doing nothing is NOT an option!

EXHIBIT G.7

Student Handout for Self-Conference Checklist

Self-Conference Checklist

If you are not able to check an item, this indicates an area you should try to improve.

___ 1. The topic is interesting to my audience (students and teachers in this class).

___ 2. The title is catchy; it grabs the reader's attention.

___ 3. The opening paragraph makes the reader want to keep reading.

___ 4. The writing flows smoothly and/or uses an effective organizational pattern.

___ 5. The message is clear. The reader is not confused about what the writer means in any part of the piece.

___ 6. The writing contains strong details or examples, including concrete language. In other words, the piece is appropriately descriptive.

___ 7. Nouns and verbs are as specific as possible, and most verbs are active verbs.

___ 8. The writer demonstrates a distinctive tone or voice.

___ 9. No distracting errors in grammar, usage, spelling, capitalization, and punctuation appear in the paper. If so, the writer will have to edit again.

10. Questions or concerns the writer still has:

Notes from conferences with the teacher:

_____

_____

_____

_____

_____

Student Handout: Preparing for a Conference with the Teacher

Preparing for a Conference with the Teacher

1. Read your draft carefully. You may want to go to a quiet area of the room and read it softly aloud to yourself. Take a pen or pencil with you and make any changes you want to make as you are reading.

2. What are your favorite parts of the piece? Why are they your favorites?

3. What parts do you think are not working well? Why are they not working well?

4. Do you have questions that you need answers to before you continue writing? If so, what are they?

Make sure you have this sheet handy when the teacher meets with you.

EXHIBIT G.9

Personal Spelling List

Personal Spelling List

With both middle and high school students, I've used a handout called a personal spelling list. It basically looks like this:

Word, spelled correctly	Practice	Practice	Practice	Hint to help me remember the correct spelling

I make enough rows for the student to be able to put about twenty words on the front side of this handout if necessary. When students receive a graded final draft back from me, any words I've noted with a circle (the proofreader's symbol for misspelling) need to go on the personal spelling list (unless they are very obscure words or proper nouns or I've asked them not to document them for some other reason). The act of writing the word four times correctly can help the students practice the correct pattern and perhaps start unlearning the incorrect pattern they have been using. (Some students would continue to practice additional times on the back of the handout, which I purposely left blank for that purpose.)

In a non-English language arts class, this handout could become the very last page in a student binder, or it can be trimmed to fit the inside back cover of a spiral notebook or composition book, into which it can be glued or taped. In these ways, it's always pretty handy. A content-area teacher may want to focus on some of the critical vocabulary in the discipline and have students practice those words—again, only if those words are showing up repeatedly misspelled in writing that has gone through multiple drafts. The personal spelling list practice sheet should not be used with long lists of words to be learned out of context or with every word a student may misspell. It is for high-frequency and high-utility words in your subject area.

Here is what a partially completed personal spelling list might look like:

Word, spelled correctly	Practice	Practice	Practice	Hint to help me remember the correct spelling
opportunity	opportunity	opportunity	opportunity	It has two Os and two Ps but only one U (so I'll stop putting a U where the 2nd O goes)
millennium	millennium	millennium	millennium	Like the word "annual," it has two Ns. They both come from the Latin word meaning "year."

EXHIBIT G.10

Personal Conventions List

Personal Conventions List

Here is what a student might have on this handout after a class mini-lesson on the frequently confused words there, their, and they're:

Convention: What is the rule?	The problem: How it was used incorrectly	How to fix the problem	My own example of using it correctly	Hint to help me remember the rule
THERE is an adverb. THEIR shows possession. THEY'RE is a contraction.	Part of the reason for extinction is because of a lack of proper food their.	Part of the reason for extinction is because of a lack of proper food THERE. (There is a place.)	The animals lived THERE. THEIR babies could not live because of a lack of food. THEY'RE all now extinct.	When I see "they're" or want to use it, I will say "they are" in the sentence and see if that makes sense. If not, it's one of the other two. If something does not belong to someone in the sentence, then I don't need "their." If I do those two things and they don't fit, I probably need "there."

Obviously, non-English teachers want to preserve the use of the personal conventions sheet (especially with whole-class mini-lessons) for serious and/or heavily repeated errors. This particular tool, the conventions list, is a wonderful tool about which to collaborate with other teachers on your team or with the English teachers who teach your students. When certain errors like the ubiquitous there/their/they're or its/it's usage error or the frequency of sentence fragments are appearing in more than 25 percent of student papers repeatedly, a team effort to address these conventions may be in order. If you carefully track the student writing data, you will notice that a team approach can result in dramatic improvement in a very short time.

EXHIBIT G.11

Student Handout for Peer Editing

Peer Editing

Today we will be involved in a peer editing process. You will swap drafts with someone. Follow the steps below, using a colored pencil or marker if possible so that your marks and notes will be obvious to the writer.

1. Circle every end mark (period, question mark, or exclamation point) or put them in as needed and then circle them. This helps the writer check for fragments and run-ons.

2. Circle every word that may be misspelled. It's the writer's job to find the correct spelling, not yours. If you circle something that is spelled correctly, the writer will disregard your circle.

3. Put a check mark in the margin of any line that contains a good example, image, word, or phrase—something that really catches the reader's attention. Explain this to the writer out loud or write comments in the margin.

4. Put a question mark in the margin of any line that has something unclear. Explain this to the writer verbally or in writing.

5. Draw a square around every form of the verb "be" and all passive voice verbs. The writer needs to make these more specific and active if possible. If you have suggestions, explain them aloud to the writer or make notes in the margin.

6. Underline any "tired" or overused words/phrases and suggest alternatives by writing them in above the originals.

APPENDIX H: **Writing Assignments for a High School Chemistry Class**

EXHIBIT H.1	Report Evaluation

Chemistry

Name _____

Date _____ Due _____

Octogenarian Report Evaluation

Points/Possible	Performance Criteria
_____ 10	**Thesis/objective apparent and main points of thesis supported:** Clearly stated in introduction and easy to find in paper.
_____ 10	**Informal Documentation:** Information not originating with the student author is documented. "Documented," or "cited" means it is: 1. Identified as coming from the interviewee, interviewee is identified. 2. Paraphrased or quoted from interviewee or credible literature. 3. (Formal documentation optional) Designated with citation as coming from another source via Internet address, or MLA or APA format.
_____ 10	**Scientific Review:** There appears to be some information presented either from the textbook or another credible source to support thesis. (You may also gather as much background information on the history of petroleum products in the United States.)
_____ 20	**Evidence of knowledge of petroleum products and use as outlined in objective of report:** Student correctly applies concepts, and specific information to compare the use of petroleum now and in the 1930s and 40s. Student offers suggestions as to what might be important for future generations to learn regarding the pre-petroleum product age.
_____ 20	**Analysis: Information/Content:** Student provides reasonable analysis through comparisons between today and 50 plus years ago. Conclusion is justified. Thesis is directly supported. Analysis includes explanation of limitations in conclusion.
_____ 10	**Structure of paper:** Student uses logical order and organization. Main points are clear with adequate transitions between ideas.
_____ 10	**Style:** Paper is interesting, and easy to read. It has a low fog index.
_____ 10	**Mechanics:** correct grammar, spelling, and use of conventions.

	Comments:
	
	Total Points Possible
	    90-100 = A
	    80-89 = B
	    70-79 = C

EXHIBIT H.2

Self/Peer Evaluation

Name _____

Date _____ Due _____

Octogenarian Report – Self/Peer Evaluation Form
(to be completed by student and separately by 2 peers)

Clear Purpose	Yes = ✓ No = ?	Comments
Did the writer meet the objective: Did writer address whether petroleum is used to build other molecules or products and that it is used as fuel? Did author discuss how petroleum is a nonrenewable resource and how our supplies are not expected to last forever, or might become too expensive to use as we do today? 1. How does the use of petroleum in the 1930s and 1940s compare to our uses today? 2. What can we learn from people who were alive prior to the widespread use of petroleum products that might help us in the future? Address these questions when you write your essay and use the interview as research to support your thesis.		
Information/Content		
Does the information support thesis? Is support adequately detailed or technical? Is there anything irrelevant in this paper? Does the paper show reasonable effort and adequate understanding? Are the sources of information accurate and appropriate?		
Structure		
Introduction includes general information followed by a thesis. Main points are clear, well supported. Adequate transitions between ideas are present, making the reading easy to follow. Conclusion summarizes key points.		
Style		
Is the point of view consistent? Is technical vocabulary defined? Sufficient detail is evident through use of descriptive phrases. Low fog index.		
Mechanics/ Grammar		
Correct use of grammar. Conventions used properly. Spelling has been checked/corrected.		

Evaluation by _____

Date _____

Printed name _____

EXHIBIT H.3

Student Example of an Octogenarian Report

Octogenarian Report

In order to learn more about life before petroleum and petroleum products I decided to interview my grandfather. My grandfather lived on a farm with his brother and three sisters and his parents. They had a two story farm house on a ninety acre self sufficient farm. On the arm they grew strawberries and plums and also had an orchard a few cows' chickens pigs and horses.

When traveling he would walk or ride his bike or horse. As a family they would ride a horse and buggy. He rode a steam train into Portland a few times and never traveled far very often. In 1918 they got a car, which they rode into Portland and to forest grove for shopping.

For heating and lighting they had a wood stove and coal oil lamps. They had to cut lots of wood for the stove and some more wood for a prune dryer. The prunes were their main income and the dryer took a large amount of wood at some point they got oxyacetylene gas lights feed by a carbide and water tank (carbide reacts with water to create acetylene oxygen is add to the gas just before it leaves the fixture.).They finally got electricity after my grandfather moved away.

Cleaning was difficult so it was much less common then it is today. They used homemade soap and had to bath in a large washtub but they did wash their faces every day. There was a reservoir behind the wood stove for hot water though there was not much water in it. In order to clean clothing they had a washboard and at some point they got a hand-cranked washer.

In order to store food caning, salting and drying food was very necessary for foods that spoil. They had an icebox for temporary storage but the ice in it would melt after a few days and they would have to buy more.

Entertainment wise they had a battery operated radio, and they would play in the woods swim in the creek or ride bikes in the winter they could go ice-skating sledding and even skiing at David hill sometimes. They were the only family in the area that had a radio so all their neighbors would come over when there was a big game or fight on that night.

In closing life before petroleum was much harder than life today because do any thing took more effort. Since there were no easy sources of energy you had to chop wood. Without plastics and refrigerators storing food took a lot of effort. With the cars they had at that time and no airplanes travel was more difficult and less common. Also because people had to work so much you had very little free time and fewer ways to spend it.

APPENDIX I: **Research Writing**

EXHIBIT I.1

Cornell Notes Page as a Note-Taking Template for Research

Cornell Notes for Research Writing

Sources used:

1. _____

Remember to include title, author, date of publication, place of publication or Internet address, and volume and page numbers if appropriate.

2. _____

3. _____

Key points in the information	Relevant details for my report

Summary of information above (my own words):

EXHIBIT I.2

Student Handout for I-Search Paper

Planning Your I-Search Paper

Answer the following so that I will have more information about your research. I will use your answers to make suggestions and to approve your plan.

1. Explain your topic in a sentence or two.

2. What materials do you plan to read? Please give specific titles that you have seen in the media center and/or online, and tell what kind of resource each is (for example, book, magazine, Internet site, etc.).

3. What materials and/or people do you plan to watch? Please give specific titles that you have already located, and tell what kind of resource each is (for example, clip on YouTube, video documentary, speech, presentation, etc.).

4. List at least three questions that you want to ask someone about.

      1.

      2.

      3.

5. Name at least one person, either by name or by his or her role, of whom you could ask these questions. (See me if you need suggestions.)

6. Is there something active that you plan to do during or after your research phase (for example, complete a community service project, attend a school board meeting, etc.)? If so, describe it.

EXHIBIT I.3

Multi-Genre Research

The Multi-Genre Research Project
English II
Mrs. Peery

This project is to be completed mainly for homework; however, you are also welcome to work on it in class during any writing workshop periods. All written portions are due January 7 and must be word-processed following the final draft guidelines you have in your notebook.

You will present your project in class on January 8 or 9. Your presentation must be five to ten minutes long. More specific guidelines for the presentation will be discussed in class later.

1. Choose a person, event, or issue that is historically significant. Mr. Moorhead and Mrs. Peery must approve your topic by December 9.

   Examples:

   Person—Napoleon, Thomas Jefferson, Adolf Hitler, Albert Einstein, Thurgood Marshall, Mother Teresa, Nelson Mandela

   Event—World War II, the Holocaust, the Vietnam War, the sinking of the Titanic, the U.S. landing on the moon

   Issue—AIDS, apartheid, child labor, space exploration, immigration

2. Research your topic by finding information in at least four of the following sources: encyclopedias, magazines, newspapers, the Internet, historical fiction books, nonfiction books, reports, songs, poems, television/video programs, radio recordings, and interviews of people who know about your topic. Use interesting sources—not just easy ones to find!

   Research requirements:

   a. Four or more different kinds of sources used

   b. No more than half of your information from the Internet unless you have prior approval of Mr. Moorhead or Mrs. Peery

   c. Full documentation of each source in a bibliography or works cited list to be submitted with your project. See the *Writers Inc.* book for further information about your citations.

3. Write about your topic in at least three genres. Examples: poem, song, short story, narrative essay, editorial, letter, speech, interview (real or imagined), news article, dialogue, drama, script, children's picture book, comic strip, editorial cartoon. You may suggest another genre or form of writing to Mrs. Peery for possible approval.

EXHIBIT I.4

Giving PowerPoint Presentations

Student Handout

PowerPoint Presentation Based on Research

You will be creating a PowerPoint presentation based on the research you are conducting in our class.

Guidelines for Research:

1. Your information should come from a minimum of three sources beyond our textbooks.

2. Use the Cornell research notes page to document your sources and record important information.

Guidelines for the PowerPoint Presentation:

1. Create a minimum of five slides.

2. Use no more than two fonts in the presentation (one for headings, one for text).

3. All headings should be at least size 44. All other text should be at least size 24. All text should be in bold for easy viewing.

4. Include a works cited (references) slide at the end. This slide does not count toward the minimum of five slides. This slide must follow the citation guidelines you have been given in class.

5. A storyboard or flow chart of your PowerPoint must be submitted by _____. After I approve this plan, you may begin designing the PowerPoint.

6. Your presentation should be eight to twelve minutes in length. We will discuss specifics for this presentation after all storyboards/flow charts are approved and students begin working on their designs.

References

Ainsworth, Larry. 2003. *Unwrapping the standards: A simple process to make standards manageable.* Englewood, Colo.: Lead and Learn Press.

Allen, Janet. 2004. *Tools for teaching content literacy.* Portland, Maine: Stenhouse.

Atwell, Nancie. 1998. *In the middle: New understanding about writing, reading, and learning.* Portsmouth, N.H.: Heinemann.

Bangert-Drowns, R.L., M.M. Hurley, and B. Wilkinson. 2004. "The effects of school-based writing-to-learn interventions on academic achievement: A meta-analysis." *Review of Educational Research* 74(1): 29–58.

Calkins, Lucy. 1994. *The art of teaching writing.* Portsmouth, N.H.: Heinemann.

Claggett, Fran, L. Reid, and R. Vinz. 1996. *Recasting the text: Inquiry-based activities for comprehending and composing.* Portsmouth, N.H.: Boynton/Cook.

College Board. 2008. *Writing.* Available online at http://www.collegeboard.com/student/testing/sat/prep_one/writing.html and http://www.collegeboard.com/highered/ra/sat_faqs.html#quest3.

College Board. "Press releases." Available online at http://www.collegeboard.com/press/releases/150054.html.

Colorado Department of Education. *CSAP scoring information: Links to writing rubrics.* Available online at http://www.cde.state.co.us/cdeassess/documents/csap/csap_scoring.html#Writing.

"Common proofreading symbols." Available online at http://www.ccc.commnet.edu/writing/symbols.htm (accessed October 24, 2008).

Fletcher, Ralph, and Joann Portalupi. 2001. *Nonfiction craft lessons: Teaching information writing K-8.* Portland, Maine: Stenhouse.

Florida Department of Education. *FCAT writing rubric grade 8.* Available online at http://fcat.fldoe.org/pdf/rubrcw08.pdf.

Gardner, Howard. 1993. *Frames of mind: The theory of multiple intelligences.* New York, N.Y.: Basic Books.

Graham, Steve, and Dolores Perin. 2007. "A meta-analysis of writing instruction for adolescent students." *Journal of Educational Psychology* 99(3): 445–476.

Hillocks, George J. 1987. "Synthesis of research on teaching writing." *Educational Leadership* 44(8): 71–82.

Hyerle, David, ed. 2004. *Student successes with Thinking Maps®: School-based research, results, and models for achievement using visual tools.* Thousand Oaks, Calif.: Corwin Press.

ImagineEasy. "EasyBib." 2001–2008. Available online at http://easybib.com/.

Inspiration Software, Inc. "Inspiration demo." Available online at http://kidspiration.com/Freetrial.

Keys, Carolyn W. 1999. "Revitalizing instruction in scientific genres: Connecting knowledge production with writing to learn in science." *Science Education* 83(2):115–130.

Klentschy, Michael, Leslie Garrison, and Olga Maia Amaral. 2000. *Valle Imperale Project in Science (VIPS).* National Science Foundation Grant #ESI-9731274.

Lead and Learn Press. View online at www.leadandlearn.com/wtl/resources.

Learn NC. Available online at http://www.learnnc.org/lp/pages/2726.

Macrorie, Ken. 1988. *The I-Search paper.* Portsmouth, N.H.: Boynton/Cook Publishers.

Marzano, Robert J., Debra J. Pickering, and Jane E. Pollock. 2001. *Classroom instruction that works: Research-based strategies for increasing student achievement.* Alexandria, Virginia: Association for Supervision and Curriculum Development.

Merriam-Webster Dictionary. Available online at http://aolsvc.merriam-webster.aol.com/home-aol.htm.

Mondschein-Leist, S.R. 1997. *A guidebook for using writing to teach across the curriculum.* Boston: Pearson Custom Publishing.

Murray, Donald. 1982. *Learning by teaching.* Portsmouth, N.H.: Heinemann.

National Assessment of Educational Progress. 2007 Writing Results. Available online at http://nces.ed.gov/nationsreportcard/writing/.

National Commission on Writing. The Neglected "R". Available online at http://www.writingcommission.org/prod_downloads/writingcom/neglectedr.pdf.

National Council of Teachers of English. Available online at http://www.ncte.org/edpolicy/writing/research/122398.htm.

National Council of Teachers of English. 2008. *NCTE principles: The teaching of writing.* Available online at http://www.ncte.org/edpolicy/writing/about/122369.htm (accessed October 24, 2008).

National Council of Teachers of English. 2005. *The impact of the SAT and ACT timed writing tests.* Available online at http://www.ncte.org/library/files/About_NCTE/Press_Center/SAT/SAT-ACT-tf-report.pdf.

National Council of Teachers of Mathematics. Available online at www.nctm.org.

National Council of Teachers of Mathematics. 2008. *Executive summary: Principles and standards for school mathematics.* Available online at http://www.nctm.org/execsummary.aspx.

National Endowment for the Arts. 2004. *Reading at risk: A survey.* Available online at http://www.arts.gov/pub/ReadingatRisk.pdf.

National Science Teachers Association. *NSTA Position Statement: Assessment.* Available online at http://www.nsta.org/about/positions/assessment.aspx.

National Writing Project. 2007. "Americans believe writing skills are more important than ever." Available online at http://www.nwp.org/cs/public/print/resource/2389.

Newell, George. 1984. "Learning from writing in two content areas: A case study protocol analysis." *Research in the Teaching of English* (18): 205–287.

New York State Education Department. *Information booklet for scoring the Regents comprehensive examination in English.* Available online at http://www.emsc.nysed.gov/osa/hsgen/det541e-608.pdf.

North Carolina Public Schools, Department of Public Instruction, State Board of Education, Division of Instructional Services. *Writing across the curriculum.* Available online at http://www.ncpublicschools.org/docs/curriculum/languagearts/secondary/writing/writinghandbook.pdf (accessed October 24, 2008).

Northwest Regional Educational Laboratory. 2007. *6+1 trait writing.* Available online at http://www.nwrel.org/assessment/scoring.php?odelay=3&d=1&r=6#definition.

Northwest Regional Educational Laboratory. 2007. *6+1 trait writing: Trait definitions.* Available online at http://www.nwrel.org/assessment/definitions.php?odelay=%203&d=1.

Nussbaum, E. Michael, CarolAnne M. Kardash, and Steve Graham (eds). 2005. "The effects of goal instructions and text on the generation of counterarguments during writing." *Journal of Educational Psychology* 97(2): 157–169.

Pauk, Walter, and J. Q. Ross. 2006. *How to Study in College*, 8th ed. Boston: Houghton Mifflin.

Reeves, Douglas B. 2000. *Accountability in action: A blueprint for learning organizations.* Englewood, Colo.: Lead and Learn Press.

Reeves, Douglas B. 2002. *Reason to write: Help your child succeed in school and life through better reasoning and clear communication.* Kaplan.

Robb, Laura. Interview. Available online at http://content.scholastic.com/browse/article.jsp?id=4490.

Romano, Tom. 1995. *Writing with passion: Life stories, multiple genres.* Portsmouth, N.H.: Heinemann.

Santa, Carol M. 1988. *Content reading including study systems: Reading, writing and studying across the curriculum*: Dubuque, Iowa: Kendall/Hunt.

Sebranek , Patrick, Verne Meyer, and Dave Kemper. 1997. *Write for college: A student handbook.* Wilmington, Mass.: Great Source Publishing.

Sebranek, Patrick, Dave Kemper, and Verne Meyer. 2001. *Writers Inc.: A student handbook for writing and learning.* Wilmington, Mass.: Great Source Educational Group.

South Carolina HSAP extended response scoring rubric. Available online at http://ed.sc.gov/agency/offices/assessment/PACT/ERrubric032204.doc.

Starr, Linda. 2006. "How to write a five-paragraph essay." *Education World.* Available online at http://www.education-world.com/a_curr/profdev/profdev109.shtml.

Stead, Tony. 2001. *Is that a fact? Teaching nonfiction writing K-3.* Portland, Maine: Stenhouse.

The Houghton Mifflin Company. 2008. *The write source.* Available online at www.thewritesource.com.

Virginia Department of Education. *Virginia standards of learning assessments; Blueprint grade 8 writing test.* Available online at http://www.doe.virginia.gov/VDOE/Assessment/EnglishBlueprint05/BlueprintsG8writing.pdf.

Warlick, David, and The Landmark Project. 2006. *Landmarks son of citation machine.* Available online at http://citationmachine.net/.

Washington Office of Superintendent of Public Instruction. *Writing assessment.* Available online at http://www.k12.wa.us/assessment/WASL/Writing/resources.aspx.

Index